D1550543

Teen Sex

Teen Sex

Other books in the At Issue series:

Teen Sex

Christine Watkins, *Book Editor*

Bruce Glassman, *Vice President*
Bonnie Szumski, *Publisher*
Helen Cothran, *Managing Editor*

GREENHAVEN PRESS
An imprint of Thomson Gale, a part of The Thomson Corporation

THOMSON
™
GALE

Detroit • New York • San Francisco • San Diego • New Haven, Conn.
Waterville, Maine • London • Munich

For more information, contact
Greenhaven Press
27500 Drake Rd.
Farmington Hills, MI 48331-3535
Or you can visit our Internet site at http://www.gale.com

LIBRARY OF CONGRESS CATALOGING-IN-PUBLICATION DATA

Teen sex / Christine Watkins, book editor.
    p. cm. — (At issue)
Includes bibliographical references and index.
ISBN 0-7377-2426-9 (lib. : alk. paper) — ISBN 0-7377-2427-7 (pbk. : alk. paper)
    1. Teenagers—United States—Sexual behavior. 2. Sexual ethics for teenagers—United States. 3. Sex instruction for teenagers—United States. 4. Hygiene, Sexual—United States. I. Watkins, Christine, 1951– . II. At issue (San Diego, Calif.)
HQ27.T387 2005
306.7'0835—dc22   2004054288

Printed in the United States of America

Contents

Introduction

Many teenagers today are sexually active. One out of ten adolescents reports losing his or her virginity before the age of thirteen—a 15 percent increase since 1997. Two-thirds are sexually active by the end of high school. This sexual activity results in negative consequences for many teens. According to the Family Research Council, roughly 3 million teenagers contract a sexually transmitted disease (STD) every year. Teenage girls have the highest rate of gonorrhea infection, and unfortunately 80 percent of girls who are infected have no symptoms until the bacteria that caused it have already done serious damage. According to a United Nations report, half of the forty thousand Americans infected with HIV annually are young people under the age of twenty-five. And despite a decrease in the teen birthrate, the Centers for Disease Control and Prevention estimates that almost a million teens become pregnant each year. Studies have also shown that teens have many regrets about becoming sexually active, and the majority wish they had waited until they were older. As Tamara Kreinin, former president and CEO of the Sexuality Information and Education Council of the United States remarked, "The stakes have never been higher. Teen pregnancy is a tragedy, and AIDS is a death sentence."

Given the serious consequences of teen sex, many people are concerned about finding ways to prevent adolescents from making decisions that will hurt their physical and mental health, alter their lives forever, and sometimes even result in potentially fatal diseases. Most people who work in the field of adolescent sexual behavior support abstinence for teens—particularly younger teens—as the only certain way to prevent unplanned pregnancies and STDs. However, experts differ in their views about the best way to convince teens to refrain from sexual activity or at least to postpone it. Some advocate abstinence-until-marriage programs, which teach young people to save sex for marriage and do not provide information about contraception except to point out its failure rate. The programs include topics such as self-esteem building, character education, and self-control.

Champions of abstinence-only education believe that giving kids information about sex actually leads to sexual activity. A report by Heritage Foundation researcher Robert Rector supports this view. He describes studies of ten abstinence-only programs across the nation that found that students who participated in such curricula become less sexually active than those who had not.

On the other hand, many researchers are concerned that the abstinence-only approach leaves teenagers who do become sexually active without the knowledge of contraception that could protect them from pregnancy and disease. For example, Yale and Columbia universities carried out a six-year national study of twelve thousand teens who took virginity pledges. Findings released in April 2004 revealed that among those who had taken pledges, 85 percent admitted having had sexual intercourse before marriage despite their pledges. The study also found that teens who pledged virginity contracted STDs at about the same rate as teens who had not made such pledges and were less likely to recognize that they had a disease.

While abstinence is clearly the safest route to avoid unwanted pregnancy and disease, the fact remains that more than half of U.S. teens do become sexually active. As a result, proponents of comprehensive sex education argue that they need detailed information about sex, contraception, and STDs, including HIV/AIDS. Comprehensive sex education includes lessons on the human reproductive system and contraception as well as on the responsibilities and consequences of sexual relationships. These programs also stress the value of abstinence and teach students how to reject sexual advances. According to Planned Parenthood's *How to Talk with Your Child About Sexuality: A Parent's Guide:*

> Information does not encourage kids to be sexually active. Kids make better decisions about sex when they have all the information they need. . . . And knowledge helps them protect themselves against pregnancy and disease when they do decide to have sex.

Although experts disagree about what type of sex education is best, they do agree with most teens on one thing: Parental involvement is a key factor in determining teenagers' sexual behavior. In his book *The Other Parent*, James P. Steyer writes:

> There's a reason we have child labor laws. There's a

reason we don't let people under sixteen drive cars. There's a reason we have strict underage drinking laws—because kids are not equipped with the same capacity for judgment and discrimination as adults. They need guidance, education, and special rules to keep them from being damaged or exploited.

Parents are in a unique position to provide that guidance.

Teens say parents influence their decisions about sex more than friends or any other source. A 2003 survey conducted for the National Campaign to Prevent Teen Pregnancy found that almost nine out of ten teens believe it would be easier for them to postpone sexual activity if they could have honest discussions about sex with their parents. Virginia Gilbert, a contributing writer for the family Web site iParenting.com, interviewed five teenagers for her article "The New Teens: Sexually Informed and Responsible." She found that the three teens who had remained virgins had at least one parent with whom they felt comfortable talking about sex. One of these teens stated, "My parents were always open about sex. I never felt pressured one way or another." In contrast, the teenager from the interview who had the least open relationship with his parents was the only one currently having sex. He said, "My parents hate sex. I can't ever talk to them about it or they kill me."

Other research affirms that there is a correlation between parental involvement and the postponement of teen sexual activity. The National Longitudinal Study of Adolescent Health analyzed more than five thousand adolescents and their mothers for one year. The study found that when girls shared open and honest communication with their mothers, they were more likely to report that they had not had sexual intercourse. Furthermore, teens who felt that their mothers would disapprove of them having sexual intercourse were more likely to delay intercourse. However, parents may not realize how much they can affect their children's decisions about sex. According to Bill Albert, spokesman for the National Campaign to Prevent Teen Pregnancy, "Parents continue to underestimate the influence they have" on whether their child becomes sexually active.

1

Teen Sex: An Overview

Anna Mulrine

Anna Mulrine is a reporter for U.S. News & World Report.

Although fewer teens are having sexual intercourse than in years past, they are now dabbling in risky "anything but intercourse" sexual behaviors at increasingly young ages. As many as half of teens ages thirteen to nineteen say they have had oral sex. Fifteen percent of the teen population has been diagnosed with herpes and human papillomavirus (which can cause genital warts). These alarming figures add urgency to the debate over sex education. One side favors teaching teens to abstain from sex, but this message may not prevent them from engaging in oral and anal sex, which they do not consider real sex. The opposing side in the debate advocates more comprehensive sex education that covers detailed information about contraception and treatment for sexually transmitted diseases (STDs).

Kate, Lara, and Lynn place their orders at a Princeton, N.J., pizza parlor (plain slices, Diet Cokes all around), share a tiny pot of strawberry lip balm, and settle in for an afternoon chat.

"Now that we've had sex, my boyfriend says I'm being a tease if I'm too tired and just want to kiss," says Kate, a pert blond in a hooded Abercrombie sweatshirt.

"Yessss!" they all chime in. "I was just having that exact conversation with my boyfriend. Once you have sex, every time you hook up, you have sex," adds Lara, who also wonders whether "it's normal, the way he talks to me. He does have a temper and stuff."

These are high school sophomores, 15 years old.

Oral sex? "When I was younger"—a fifth grader, Kate clarifies—"it was kind of a slutty thing to do. But now, it's like everyone's at least having oral sex," she says. Having taken the morning-after pill twice, Kate is the expert among her girlfriends. "Freshmen might wait up to a year, sophomores wait, at most, a couple of months."

"It's like an added base," explains Lara. (All three girls asked that their names be changed.)

"Like shortstop or something," says Lynn, who is a virgin. She seeks out her housekeeper to talk about sex because "I asked both of my parents, and they wouldn't answer my questions."

> **//** *She seeks out her housekeeper to talk about sex because 'I asked both of my parents, and they wouldn't answer my questions.'* **//**

And yet, these are questions that are becoming ever more urgent. Kids from all walks of life are having sex at younger and younger ages—nearly 1 in 10 reports losing his or her virginity before the age of 13, a 15 percent increase since 1997, according to the Centers for Disease Control and Prevention [CDC]. Some 16 percent of high school sophomores have had four or more sexual partners. One in four sexually active teens will contract a sexually transmitted disease, or STD, according to the Alan Guttmacher Institute. And despite a solid 20 percent decrease in the teen birthrate between 1991 and 1999, 20 percent of sexually active girls 15 to 19 get pregnant each year, according to the Henry J. Kaiser Family Foundation. . . .

Teens are dabbling in risky behaviors

What nearly everyone agrees on is that STD's and risky "anything but intercourse" behaviors are rampant among teens—and that what to do about it is a very complicated question. Across the country, clinicians report rising diagnoses of herpes and human papillomavirus, or HPV (which can cause genital warts), which are now thought to affect 15 percent of the teen population. Girls 15 to 19 have higher rates of gonorrhea than any other age group. One quarter of all new HIV cases occur in those under the age of 21. "It's a serious epidemic," says Lloyd Kolbe, director of the CDC's Adolescent and School Health program. "We're worried."

At the Health Interested Teens' Own Program on Sexuality (HiTOPS) clinic in Princeton, the only adolescent health clinic in the state of New Jersey, Monday is the busiest day of the week, as teens flock in after coed sleepovers and weekend trysts. Fortunately, says Claire Lindberg, a nurse at the clinic, her most common diagnosis is "nothing to worry about." That's what Kate was told when she recently went to the clinic, afraid she might have contracted an STD from her boyfriend, whom she suspected of cheating. But running a close second at HiTOPS are chlamydia and herpes. Lindberg has also seen "lots and lots" of abnormal Pap smears, most often caused by HPV and increasingly common among adolescents.

"Kids come in thinking they have strep," says Maria Kushner, a physician who runs a school-based adolescent health clinic in Chicago. When they find out they actually have gonorrhea of the throat, she says, "They're grossed out—and they're devastated. They have no idea that these sorts of things even exist."

> **❝** *It's not just about not having intercourse. . . . It's about saying that you're not going to play around.* **❞**

Those sorts of things, on the whole, are the result of an expansion of risky behaviors in which kids are increasingly dabbling—at increasingly young ages. According to several surveys, as many as half of teens ages 13 to 19 say they have had oral sex. "I don't think many people would quarrel with the suggestion that oral sex among young people is much higher than it was 10 years ago," says Kolbe. And most often, Kushner adds, the kids are convinced that their choices are risk free.

Then there are the teens—and preteens—too young to fathom the consequences, both emotional and physical, of their behavior. Lynn Ponton, a professor of psychiatry at the University of California–San Francisco and author of *The Sex Lives of Teenagers*, says that this early initiation into sexual behaviors is taking a toll on teens' mental health. The result, she says, can be "dependency on boyfriends and girlfriends, serious depression around breakups and cheating, lack of goals—all of these things at such young ages.". . .

What exactly is sex?

Elizabeth Walters, a nurse midwife and counselor at HiTOPS, recalls the recent visit of a mother and her 12-year-old son. "He was this sweaty soccer-jock type," she says. The mother had noticed that her son was withdrawn and irritable after sleep-away camp. "The mom kept asking questions," says Walters. Finally, as she was ferrying him from practice in the family minivan, he told her what was wrong: He had engaged in anal sex with a girl at camp. "It was all she could do to keep the car on the road," says Walters.

Increasingly, kids are turning to sexual behaviors that were once considered taboo in order to maintain their "technical virginity," says Kushner. They're getting the message that abstinence is the goal—indeed, they're placing a premium on it. More kids are reporting having less sexual intercourse. In 1999, the most recent year for which statistics are available, two thirds of graduating seniors, and 50 percent of all high schoolers, reported having engaged in intercourse, down overall from 54 percent of all high schoolers in 1991. But what's becoming clear is that their efforts often amount to a letter rather than spirit-of-the-law approach. Health workers say that kids don't seem to view many sexual behaviors as real sex. For example, some 24 percent of teens consider anal sex abstinent behavior, according to a recent North Carolina State University study. And half of all teens don't consider oral sex sex. "There has been a shift in this idea of what constitutes sex," says Claude Allen, who, as deputy secretary of health and human services, is in charge of the Bush administration's abstinence initiative. "When we ask young people, 'Have you engaged in sexual activity?' we often hear, 'Well, what do you mean by that?'"

Is the pledge of abstinence a solution?

At Promiseland church in Austin [Texas], youth pastor Ricky Poe is regularly consulted by his kids in the manner of, say, a revered referee: Is holding hands out of bounds? How about kissing? Nearly 120 of Promiseland's teens took a pledge of abstinence . . . , but Poe thought it might be a good idea to have a recommitment ceremony. . . . Some of the teens, he felt, were not quite getting the point of the earlier abstinence pledge. "They were beginning to ask if oral sex is sex, things like that." So, like leaders of many pledge groups across the country, Poe has shifted his focus from "abstinence" to "purity." "It's not just about not having intercourse," he told the teens who gathered at the front of the altar on recommitment day. "It's about saying that you're not going to play around."

Poe worries about whether his teens will hear the message and acknowledges that many won't. "We know it's the best proven way to keep the kids safe," Poe says. "But is it realistic? I tell them, 'Your youth pastor waited,'" he adds. "'And I wasn't 18—I was 23!' That gets the gasps."

Today, as many as 1 in 6 teens nationwide is estimated to have taken a virginity pledge through rapidly growing programs like True Love Waits. One widely publicized joint study from Columbia and Yale universities had good and bad news for pledgers. The teens in the study who made pledges were found to delay the age of "sexual debut" by an average of 18 months—no small feat. When the kids did have sex, however, they were less likely to use contraception.

> *It's like telling your child, 'Don't use the car,' but then leaving the keys in the Lamborghini and saying, 'But if you do, buckle up.'*

From Chicago physician Kushner's point of view, that's a common problem. "I'm seeing more and more of it: simply unsafe sex practices," she says. "The kids love the pledge stuff, they just love it. But if they do make a mistake, and it happens all the time, they're ashamed and don't want to admit it." As a result, she adds, "The kids I'm seeing just aren't using condoms." In addition, she says, "They aren't being taught how, or that it's a way to protect themselves."

That's fine with Joe McIlhaney, an obstetrician and director of the Medical Institute for Sexual Health in Austin, who believes that there has been far too much emphasis on condoms in the past. What's more, he worries that condom effectiveness has been oversold to teens. "No one is telling them how ineffective condoms are," he says. "We don't even know if they do protect—protect is the wrong word," he interrupts himself. "The primary message is that they don't eliminate the risk of any disease." Abstinence, he emphasizes, is the only surefire means of doing that. As an added incentive, McIlhaney does his part to illustrate the risks of sex. His slide shows, graphically depicting the advanced, late-stage ravages of various sexually transmitted diseases, are legendary in abstinence-only circles.

> *Abstinence-only programs aren't going to stop teen sex by not giving teens information about how to use contraceptives.*

For his part, Allen at Health and Human Services considers discussion of contraceptives to be "inappropriate." It amounts to "mixing messages, of not giving a clear direction of what's expected behavior," he says. "It's like telling your child, 'Don't use the car,' but then leaving the keys in the Lamborghini and saying, 'But if you do, buckle up.'"

But Tamara Kreinin, president of the Sexuality Information and Education Council of the United States, regularly uses the same analogy—to make the opposite point. "I mean, wouldn't you want your kids to wear a seat belt?" she asks. . . .

Is comprehensive sex education the solution?

So, what about parents' interest in all of this? According to a . . . survey by the Kaiser Family Foundation, the majority of parents—81 percent—want schools to discuss the use of condoms and contraception with their children; where to go to be tested and treated for STDs; and how to sidestep unwanted sexual advances. What's more, teachers want to address these topics. But although 9 in 10 sex education instructors across the country believe that students should be taught about contraceptives in school, over one quarter report receiving explicit instructions from school boards and administrators. Today, 86 percent of school districts across the country require that sex ed curricula stress abstinence: Fifty-one percent allow contraceptives to be discussed as a means of preventing STDs, while 35 percent do not.

In counties around the country, from Santa Ana, Calif., to

Lubbock, Texas, to Wake, N.C., some parents and teens are pushing for more comprehensive sex education. In Montgomery County, Md., for example, health teachers are petitioning to be allowed to remove condoms from hermetically sealed boxes, currently required, in order to demonstrate how they are used. . . .

At the *Sex, Etc.* newsletter offices at Rutgers University in New Brunswick, N.J., the teen staffers trade stories about the kids who come looking for answers that they're not getting from parents or in school. Many of these questions revolve around contraceptives, which, they say, their friends seem to know increasingly little about. "Abstinence-only programs aren't going to stop teen sex by not giving teens information about how to use contraceptives," says Elizabeth Marchetta, 17, a *Sex, Etc.* board member. "They're trying to take away the one thing that could possibly keep kids safe," says Megan Esteves, 17. "They're numb to reality."

The debate continues

Are the teens right? "The short answer is that the jury's still out," says Douglas Kirby, the author of Emerging Answers, a report for the National Campaign to Prevent Teen Pregnancy. He found that "the few rigorous studies of abstinence-only curricula . . . to date do not show any overall effect on sexual behavior or contraceptive use." . . .

In the meantime, psychologists are trying hard to discover what makes kids more likely to have sex. A study in the journal *Pediatrics* . . . found that self-esteem and early sex were linked but had opposite effects on boys and girls. Girls with high self-esteem were more likely to abstain, while boys with high self-esteem were more likely to engage in sex. "I think it highlights the traditional double standard," says Gregory Zimet, a clinical psychologist at the University of Indiana and coauthor of the study. "Boys with high self-esteem are doing, at some level, what society expects: sowing their wild oats," he says. "Whereas with girls, it's really seen as a sign of bad character."

Teens are caught in the middle

While the Princeton girls clearly crave some parental input, only Lynn brings up the topic with her folks. "They let me be alone with my boyfriend in my room all of the time," Kate says, in a tone that sounds more puzzled than pleased. "Most of the times we've had sex was when they were home. I'd be like, 'I can't believe they don't know,'" she says. Pausing, she considers. "I guess what I'm thinking is that I just never understood how they couldn't know."

The teens also want relationship advice, but many are forced to go it alone. When Kate had a pregnancy scare last year, she sought support from her boyfriend. "I was like, 'I missed my period,'" she recalls. "He totally freaked out, saying, 'My mom's going to kill me.'" They started to discuss options. "He totally tries to be religious and swears he is so against abortion. Then he told me, 'But if you get an abortion, then it's not really me sinning.'" Kate shakes her head. "So the whole responsibility of sex is on me, but the good part of sex is all him. I have to take all of it."

Toward the end of their meal at the pizza parlor, Lynn turns to Kate.

"Are you sorry you had sex?"

"So young, you mean?" Kate asks. She sighs heavily, looks up for a moment, and begins.

"Well, it wasn't the biggest mistake of my life or anything," she says. "I mean, yeah, I regret it, but maybe I would've regretted it if I waited until I was 18. Maybe you always think you should have waited longer."

The girls nod.

Lara sips her Diet Coke. "I wonder if we'll look back on this time, like when we were in middle school, and we'd go out with boys for, like, two days and not talk to them?" she says.

"I wonder if we'll look back to now in the same way and go, 'What were we thinking?'"

Across the country, preachers and parents, teachers and legislators are hoping that it's a question tomorrow's teens won't be forced to ask.

2

Oral Sex Is the New Trend for Young Teens

Lisa Remez

Lisa Remez is associate editor of Family Planning Perspectives, *published by the Alan Guttmacher Institute, a nonprofit organization that focuses on sexual and reproductive health research, policy analysis, and public education.*

There is growing evidence, though still anecdotal, that adolescents are turning to oral sex as a way to avoid pregnancy and sexually transmitted diseases (STDs). They may also view oral sex as something less consequential than intercourse and as a sexual activity that will technically allow them to remain virgins. However, these adolescents are dangerously unaware that they can acquire and spread STDs through oral sex. Health educators who teach abstinence only are in a quandary over whether to teach students which sexual activities to abstain from because they fear that such explanations would be like providing a "how to" manual to teenagers.

The first hint in the popular press of a new "trend" in sexual activity among young people appeared in an April 1997 article in *The New York Times*. That article asserted that high school students who had come of age with AIDS education considered oral sex to be a far less dangerous alternative, in both physical and emotional terms, than vaginal intercourse. By 1999, the press reports started attributing this behavior to even younger students. A July [2000] *Washington Post* article described an "unsettling new fad" in which suburban middle-school students were regularly engaging in oral sex at one an-

Lisa Remez, "Oral Sex Among Adolescents: Is It Sex or Is It Abstinence?" *Family Planning Perspectives*, vol. 32, November 2000. Copyright © 2000 by the Alan Guttmacher Institute. Reproduced by permission.

other's homes, in parks and even on school grounds; this piece reported an oral sex prevalence estimate, attributed to un-named counselors and sexual behavior researchers, of "about half by the time students are in high school."

Middle-school students experiment with oral sex

Other stories followed, such as a piece in *Talk* magazine in February 2000 that reported on interviews with 12–16-year-olds. These students set seventh grade as the starting point for oral sex, which they claimed begins considerably earlier than intercourse. By 10th grade, according to the reporter, "well over half of their classmates were involved." This article laid part of the blame on dual-career, overworked "parents who were afraid to parent," and also mentioned that young adolescents were caught between messages about AIDS and abstinence on the one hand and the saturation of the culture with sexual imagery on the other. In April 2000, another *New York Times* article on precocious sexuality quoted a Manhattan psychologist as saying "it's like a goodnight kiss to them" in a description of how seventh- and eighth-grade virgins who were saving themselves for marriage were having oral sex in the meantime because they perceived it to be safe and risk-free.

> *// Suburban middle-school students were regularly engaging in oral sex at one another's homes, in parks and even on school grounds. //*

In a July 2000 *Washington Post Magazine* cover story, eighth graders described being regularly propositioned for oral sex in school. The reporter echoed the assertion made in earlier articles that although overall sexual activity among older, high school–aged adolescents—as measured by the proportion who have ever had penile-vaginal intercourse—seemed to have recently leveled off or slightly declined, middle-school-aged students (aged 12–14) appeared to be experimenting with a wider range of behaviors at progressively younger ages. . . .

Experts believe that the type of oral sex practiced by young teenagers is overwhelmingly fellatio, not cunnilingus. Accord-

ing to Deborah Tolman, senior research scientist at the Wellesley Center for Research on Women, that distinction is para-
mount: "We are not fainting in the street because boys are giving girls cunnilingus. Which is not to say that girls and boys
never have that experience. They probably do, and just rarely
do it again for a really long time, because of how girls feel about
themselves and their bodies, how boys feel about girls' bodies,
and the misinformation they have about each other's bodies."

Oral sex can lead to STDs

Many STDs [sexually transmitted diseases] can be transmitted
by either fellatio or cunnilingus, although some are more easily passed than others. According to Penelope Hitchcock, chief
of the Sexually Transmitted Diseases Branch of the National Institute of Allergy and Infectious Diseases, saliva tends to inacti-
vate the HIV virus, so while transmission through oral intercourse is not impossible, it is relatively rare. Other viral STDs
that can be transmitted orally include human papillomavirus,
herpes simplex virus and hepatitis B, while gonorrhea, syphilis,
chlamydia and chancroid are among the bacterial infections
that can be passed through oral sex.

In the absence of survey data on the frequency of oral sex,
the question arises as to whether clinicians are seeing evidence
of a rise in STDs that have been acquired orally. The answer de-
pends upon the person asked. Some say they have seen no
change in STDs acquired noncoitally, while others report that
they are seeing both new types of infections and new types of
patients—i.e., teenagers who have not yet initiated coitus but
who come in with fears and anxiety over having acquired an
infection orally.

> *I have more patients who are virgins who
> report to me that they are worried about STDs they
> may have gotten by having oral sex.*

Linda Dominguez, assistant medical director of Planned Parenthood of New Mexico and a nurse practitioner with a private
practice, reports that at patients' requests, she is performing
more oral swabs and throat inspections now than in the past.

She affirms that "I have more patients who are virgins who report to me that they are worried about STDs they may have gotten by having oral sex. There are a lot of questions and concerns about herpes, since they seem to know that there is some risk of 'top and bottom' herpes, as one of my patients put it."

Sharon Schnare, a family planning clinician and consultant in Seattle, remarks that she now sees many teenagers with oral herpes. She adds that "I have also found, though rarely, oral Condylomata acuminata [a sexually transmitted condition caused by the human papillomavirus] in teenagers." Moreover, Hitchcock states that "several studies have shown that one-third of the isolates from genital herpes cases in kids right now are HSV1 [herpes simplex virus 1, the oral strain], which suggests a significant amount of oral intercourse is going on." This suggestion is impossible to verify, however, because of the extensive crossover between the two strains. Moreover, trends are especially hard to detect because of past and current problems in the reliability of type-specific testing.

> *Middle-school girls sometimes look at oral sex as an absolute bargain.*

Pharyngeal gonorrhea is one STD that is definitely acquired through oral sex. A few cases of pharyngeal gonorrhea have been diagnosed in adolescent girls in Dominguez's family planning clinic in New Mexico and in one region of Georgia through a community screening project among middle-school students to detect certain strains of meningitis bacteria carried in the throat. In Georgia, the cases caught everyone off guard, according to Kathleen Toomey [director of the Division of Public Health in Georgia's Department of Human Resources]. The infections were found only because throat swabs were being done for meningitis in a population that would not be considered "sexually active" in the traditional sense of the word.

Many researchers and clinicians believe that young adolescents who are having oral sex before they start coitus might be especially reluctant to seek clinical care. Moreover, adolescents virtually never use condoms or dental dams to protect against STD infection during oral sex, even those who know about the risk and worry that they might become infected. . . .

What teens think

Experts say there are multiple, interrelated reasons for why adolescents might be turning to oral sex. Deborah Roffman, a sexuality educator at The Park School in Baltimore, asserts that "middle-school girls sometimes look at oral sex as an absolute bargain—you don't get pregnant, they think you don't get diseases, you're still a virgin and you're in control since it's something that they can do to boys (whereas sex is almost always described as something boys do to girls)."

> *Oral sex is clearly seen as something very different than intercourse, as something other than sex.*

This sense of control is illusory, according to Roffman, because engaging in fellatio out of peer pressure or to gain popularity is clearly exploitative of girls who lack the maturity to realize it. The issue of just how voluntary oral sex is for many girls came up repeatedly, especially when the act is performed "to make boys happy" or when alcohol is involved. Roffman relates the experience of a guidance counselor who, after bringing up the topic of rape in this context of coerced oral sex, was told by female students that the term did not apply to their situation, because fellatio "is not really sex."

Teenagers seem to be especially misinformed about the STD risks of oral sex. Experts repeatedly mentioned their concerns over adolescents' perceptions of oral sex as less risky than intercourse, especially in the context of teenagers' tendency to have very short-term relationships. Several observers mentioned the trap of AIDS education, which often teaches that HIV is transmitted through sexual intercourse, so adolescents think they are avoiding risk by avoiding sexual intercourse. Sarah Brown, director of the National Campaign to Prevent Teen Pregnancy, suggests what some adolescents might be thinking: "Okay, we get it. You adults really don't want us to have sexual intercourse, and you're probably right because of AIDS and pregnancy. But we're still sexual and we're going to do other things."

[Sex educator Deborah] Haffner's interviews with 11th and 12th graders reveal that they view oral as "something you can do with someone you're not as intimate with, while intercourse is, by and large, reserved for that special person." This emotional differential between oral sex and vaginal sex—the assertion that oral sex carries few or no emotional ties—is acknowledged by many professionals who work with adolescents. Linda Dominguez quotes her adolescent patients as thinking "if you're going to avoid intercourse, you're going to resort to oral sex. You're going to do something that is sexual, but in some ways emotionally safer, before you give the big one away."

Adolescent health professionals reinforced the view reported in the popular press that today's adolescents consider oral sex to be less consequential and less intimate than intercourse. "Oral sex is clearly seen as something very different than intercourse, as something other than sex," according to Susan Rosenthal [a professor of pediatrics and a pediatric psychologist at Cincinnati Children's Hospital Medical Center]. . . .

Is oral sex sex?

Data collected in small-scale evaluations of abstinence education programs are an unexpected source of information on adolescents' current experience with oral sex. A few evaluation sites recently used questionnaires that asked about a variety of sexual activities in assessing how middle-school students interpret messages about behaviors to be abstained from. Thus, those who had had oral sex but not coitus could be distinguished from other groups. According to Stan Weed, director of the Institute for Research and Evaluation in Salt Lake City, the responses to these items indicate that "there is a percentage of kids for whom oral sex seems to be a substitute for intercourse; I'm guessing that, although it varies with the sample, for around 25% of the kids who have had any kind of intimate sexual activity, that activity is oral sex, not intercourse."

The many, even competing, agendas in the culturally loaded definitions of the term "sex" make sexuality research exceptionally challenging to conduct. In early fall of 1998, the American public was riveted by President Bill Clinton's claim that he had not perjured himself because he "did not have sexual relations with that woman [White House intern Monica Lewinsky]"; he had, in fact, had something else—oral sex. At the time, according to a Gallup Poll, roughly 20% of adults also believed that oral sex did not constitute "sexual relations." No one knows how many adolescents feel the same way. As Robert Blum, director of the Adolescent Health Program at the University of Minnesota puts it, "we know that there are many sexual practices other than intercourse that predispose young people to negative health outcomes. What we really don't know is, in an age of a focus on abstinence, how young people have come to understand what is meant by being sexually active.". . .

> *Adults and adolescents do not necessarily agree on what activities are now inferred by the word 'sex.'*

In the face of limited rigorous research in this area, magazines for teenagers serve as an important source of information on what adolescents think about oral sex. Impressions of oral sex are necessarily bound up with views on sexual intercourse, since one is usually cited as either a precursor or substitute for the other. According to a fall 1999 survey conducted by *Seventeen* magazine in which 723 15–19-year-old males and females were approached in malls, 49% considered oral sex to be "not as big a deal as sexual intercourse," and 40% said it did not count as "sex." A summer 2000 Internet survey conducted by *Twist* magazine received 10,000 on-line responses from 13–19-year-old girls, 18% of whom said that oral sex was something that you did with your boyfriend before you are ready to have sex; the same proportion stated that oral sex was a substitute for intercourse.

Adults and adolescents do not necessarily agree on what activities are now inferred by the word "sex." Individuals from across the ideological spectrum who were interviewed for this report acknowledged that the assumption of what "sex" encompasses has changed. As Tom Klaus, president of Legacy Resource Group in Iowa, which produces comprehensive pregnancy prevention and abstinence resources for educators, observes, "we thought we were on the same page as our kids when we talked about it. The new emerging paradigm is that we can't be so certain that we are really talking about the same thing."

What is abstinence?

If adolescents perceive oral sex as something different from sex, do they view it as abstinence? Research conducted in 1999 with 282 12–17-year-olds in rural areas in the Midwest probed how adolescents who received abstinence education interpreted the term. Students struggled to come up with a coherent definition, although older adolescents had less difficulty than younger ones. The wide-ranging responses covered ground from "kissing is probably okay" to "just no intercourse."

Some of the students brought marriage into their definition of abstinence, and others asserted that it means going only as far sexually as one wanted to or felt comfortable with. The list of behaviors encompassed within virginity was long, and typically ended in statements such as "To me, the only thing that would take away my virginity is having sex. Everything else is permitted." (The very few recent abstinence program evaluations that assessed whether adolescents had engaged in sexual activities other than intercourse did not ask whether they did under the assumption that they were being abstinent.) . . .

Health educators themselves might be unclear about precisely what the term "abstinence" means. In a 1999 e-mail survey of 72 health educators, for example, nearly one-third (30%) responded that oral sex was abstinent behavior. A similar proportion (29%), however, asserted that mutual masturbation would not qualify as abstinence.

Experts interviewed for this report acknowledged that defining what is meant by abstinence—and accurately communicating that definition to students—has become a crucial issue. While everyone agrees that the implicit meaning of the term is abstaining from vaginal-penile intercourse, especially since the concept is often taught as a "method" of avoiding pregnancy, the consensus stops there. What is the specific behavior that signals the end of abstinence and the beginning of sex? . . .

> *Health educators themselves might be unclear about precisely what the term 'abstinence' means.*

This issue is especially thorny because some abstinence-only programs are committed to being as specific as possible so adolescents do not take away the wrong message about what abstinence is, while others insist that specifying those behaviors violates a child's innocence and amounts to providing a "how-to" manual. Tom Klaus affirms that the inability to specify what activities youth should abstain from is forcing a Catch 22—adolescents cannot practice abstinence until they know what abstinence is, but in order to teach them what abstinence is, they have to be taught what sex is. According to Stan Weed, "there's no settled consensus in the abstinence movement. Some programs are willing to take it head on and say [oral sex] is not an appropriate activity, if you think this is a substitute, you're wrong; others are not even dealing with it."

> *The deeply rooted tendency to define sex as intercourse might not necessarily be working any more.*

Amy Stephens of Focus on the Family, a Colorado Springs–based conservative religious organization, asserts that in its curriculum, Sex, Lies and . . . the Truth, "our definition is refraining from all sexual activity, which includes intercourse, oral sex, anal sex and mutual masturbation—the only 100% effective means of preventing pregnancy and the spread of STDs." Stephens notes that the different faith communities will use language specific to their congregations (i.e., "chastity" in Catholic circles and "purity" in Christian Evangelical communities). In the official definition of abstinence used by the Chicago-based Project Reality, the "sexual activity" to be avoided until marriage "refers to any type of genital contact or sexual stimulation including, but not limited to, sexual intercourse."

The dilemma over sex education

Some adolescent health professionals believe that although the revelation of early oral sex has been shocking, it has had the positive effect of forcing a dialogue with adolescents about the full meaning of sexuality and of the importance of defining sex not as a single act, but as a whole range of behaviors. There is widespread agreement among educators from all along the ideological spectrum that the continuing lack of adult guidance about what sex really means contributes to the desensitized, "body-part" sex talked about in the press, whatever the real prevalence might be. They stress that teachers and parents need to do a better job at helping children interpret the context-free messages of sexuality they are bombarded with in the media, which now includes the still-evolving Internet. Some experts believe that programs are moving in the right direction by teaching adolescents how to identify bad or abusive relationships, but that there is still much work to be done to help them with intimacy and how to recognize good relationships.

The lack of guidelines on what activity is appropriate when is a common concern among professionals who work with adolescents. Educators who endorse comprehensive sexuality education support giving adolescents the criteria they need to decide when to abstain or when to participate across the full continuum of sexual behaviors. Abstinence proponents are wrestling with how to handle an evolving dilemma that pits those who stress the need to be as precise as possible in specifying the range of behaviors to be abstained from against others who insist that such specificity violates the core of abstinence-only education. . . .

What are some of the health consequences of continuing to define sex so narrowly and to lack data on a wider range of behaviors? "As public health people, we need to think about how we can address prevention and education, when we don't even know which are the behaviors we are trying to 'prevent,'" Kathleen Toomey says. She notes that the cases of pharyngeal gonorrhea were only uncovered among middle schoolers, who had not sought care otherwise, through a screening project for meningitis, adding "we're probably missing this because we are not routinely doing throat swabs and because we are not asking the right questions."

There is widespread agreement that oral STD risk in adolescent populations has yet to be adequately measured and screened for. This situation is exacerbated by the fact that many of the adolescent patients involved have not yet initiated coitus and thus are unlikely to visit a family planning or STD clinic. When they do, several practitioners assert, more detailed sexual histories, despite the extra time involved, are essential to prevent misdiagnosis and to understand what the patient, rather than the provider, means by "sexual activity." In the absence of an adequate screening protocol, unknowing clinicians might automatically assume that the patient has strep and prescribe antibiotics. The fact that many infections are asymptomatic further complicates the diagnosis when the mode of infection is not easily talked about.

The deeply rooted tendency to define sex as intercourse might not necessarily be working any more in reaching many adolescent patients at risk. How to counsel adolescents about lowering that risk is especially problematic, since many young people consider oral sex itself to be a form of risk reduction and are probably already reluctant (as are many adults) to discuss oral sex openly or to use dental dams or condoms. Many practitioners feel they have gotten very good at talking about penetrative risk, but that they now need to hone their skills at communicating with their young clients about other types of sexual activities.

3

Choosing Virginity: A New Attitude

Lorraine Ali and Julie Scelfo

Lorraine Ali is a music critic and journalist for Newsweek *magazine. She has written articles for the* Los Angeles Times, Rolling Stone, *and the* New York Times. *Julie Scelfo, a correspondent for* Newsweek *magazine, reports on society and culture.*

The number of teenagers having sex is decreasing, but the controversy over sex education has become acrimonious. Proponents of comprehensive sex education programs that provide information about contraceptives and the physical and emotional aspects of sexual activity believe that teaching abstinence is not enough. Others argue that the abstinence-until-marriage message is responsible for this "let's not" trend. When researchers asked young people why they are choosing to say no to sex, they cited self-discipline, strong family values, and a sense of empowerment as reasons.

There's a sexual revolution going on in America, and believe it or not, it has nothing to do with Christina Aguilera's bare-it-all video "Dirrty." The uprising is taking place in the real world, not on "The Real World." Visit any American high school and you'll likely find a growing number of students who watch scabrous TV shows like "Shipmates," listen to Eminem— and have decided to remain chaste until marriage. Rejecting the get-down-make-love ethos of their parents' generation, this wave of young adults represents a new counterculture, one clearly at odds with the mainstream media at their routine use of sex to boost ratings and peddle product.

According to a recent study from the Centers for Disease Control, the number of high-school students who say they've never had sexual intercourse rose by almost 10 percent between 1991 and 2001. Parents, public-health officials and sexually beleaguered teens themselves may be relieved by this "let's not" trend. But the new abstinence movement, largely fostered by cultural conservatives and evangelical Christians, has also become hotly controversial.

As the Bush administration plans to increase federal funding for abstinence programs by nearly a third, to $135 million, the Advocates for Youth and other proponents of a more comprehensive approach to sex ed argue that teaching abstinence isn't enough. Teens also need to know how to protect themselves if they do have sex, these groups say, and they need to understand the emotional intensity inherent in sexual relationships.

The debate concerns public policy, but the real issue is personal choice. At the center of it all are the young people themselves, whose voices are often drowned out by the political cacophony. Some of them opened up and talked candidly to *Newsweek* about their reasons for abstaining from sex until marriage. It's clear that religion plays a critical role in this extraordinarily private decision. But there are other factors as well: caring parents, a sense of their own unreadiness, the desire to gain some semblance of control over their own destinies. Here are their stories.

The Wellesley girl

Alice Kunce says she's a feminist, but not the "army-boot-wearing, shaved-head, I-hate-all-men kind." The curly-haired 18-year-old Wellesley College sophomore—she skipped a grade in elementary school—looks and talks like what she is: one of the many bright, outspoken students at the liberal Massachusetts women's college. She's also a virgin. "One of the empowering things about the feminist movement," she says, "is that we're able to assert ourselves, to say no to sex and not feel pressured about it. And I think guys are kind of getting it. Like, 'Oh, not everyone's doing it'."

But judging by MTV's "Undressed," UPN's "Buffy the Vampire Slayer" and just about every other TV program or movie targeted at teens, everyone is doing it. Alice grew up with these images, but as a small-town girl in Jefferson City, Mo., most teen shows felt alien and alienating. "You're either a prudish person who can't handle talking about sex or you're out every Saturday night getting some," she says. "But if you're not sexually active and you're willing to discuss the subject, you can't be called a prude. How do they market to that?" The friend from back home she's been dating since August asked not to be identified in this story, but Alice doesn't mind talking candidly about what they do—or don't do. "Which is acceptable? Oral, vaginal or anal sex?" she asks. "For me, they're all sex. In high school, you could have oral sex and still call yourself a virgin. Now I'm like, 'Well, what makes one less intimate than the other?'"

> *Parents, public-health officials and sexually beleaguered teens themselves may be relieved by this 'let's not' trend.*

Alice, a regular churchgoer who also teaches Sunday school, says religion is not the reason she's chosen abstinence. She fears STDs [sexually transmitted diseases] and pregnancy, of course, but above all, she says, she's not mature enough emotionally to handle the deep intimacy sex can bring. Though most people in her college, or even back in her Bible-belt high school, haven't made the same choice, Alice says she has never felt ostracized. If anything, she feels a need to speak up for those being coerced by aggressive abstinence groups. "Religious pressure was and is a lot greater than peer pressure," says Alice, who has never taken part in an abstinence program. "I don't think there are as many teens saying 'Oh come on, everybody's having sex' as there are church leaders saying 'No, it's bad, don't do it. It'll ruin your life.' The choices many religious groups leave you with are either no sex at all or uneducated sex. What happened to educating young people about how they can protect themselves?"

The dream team

Karl Nicoletti wasted no time when it came to having "the talk" with his son, Chris. It happened five years ago, when Chris was in sixth grade. Nicoletti was driving him home from school and the subject of girls came up. "I know many parents who are wishy-washy when talking to their kids about sex. I just said, 'No, you're not going to have sex. Keep your pecker in your pants until you graduate from high school'."

Today, the 16-year-old from Longmont, Colo., vows he'll remain abstinent until marriage. So does his girlfriend, 17-year-old Amanda Wing, whose parents set similarly strict rules for her and her two older brothers. "It's amazing, but they did listen," says her mother, Lynn Wing. Amanda has been dating Chris for only two months, but they've known each other for eight years. On a Tuesday-night dinner date at Portabello's (just across from the Twin Peaks Mall), Amanda asks, "You gonna get the chicken parmesan again?" Chris nods. "Yep. You know me well." They seem like a long-married couple—except that they listen to the Dave Matthews Band, have a 10:30 weeknight curfew and never go beyond kissing and hugging. (The guidelines set by Chris's dad: no touching anywhere that a soccer uniform covers.)

> *We're able to assert ourselves, to say no to sex and not feel pressured about it.*

"Society is so run by sex," says Chris, who looks like Madison Avenue's conception of an All-American boy in his Abercrombie sweat shirt and faded baggy jeans. "Just look at everything—TV, movies. The culture today makes it seem OK to have sex whenever, however or with whoever you want. I just disagree with that." Amanda, who looks tomboy comfy in baggy brown cords, a white T shirt and chunky-soled shoes, feels the same way. "Sex should be a special thing that doesn't need to be public," she says. "But if you're abstinent, its like you're the one set aside from society because you're not 'doing it'."

The peer pressure in this town of 71,000 people in the shadow of the Rocky Mountains is substantially less than in cosmopolitan Denver, 45 minutes away. ("It figures you had to come all the way out here to find a virgin," one local said.) Chris joined a Christian abstinence group called Teen Advisors this year. "We watched their slide show in eighth grade and it just has pictures of all these STDs," he says. "It's one of the grossest things you've ever seen. I didn't want to touch a girl, like, forever." He now goes out once a month and talks to middle schoolers about abstinence. Amanda saw the same presentation. "It's horrible," she says. "If that doesn't scare kids out of sex, nothing will." Could these gruesome images put them off sex for life? Chris and Amanda say no. They're sure that whoever they marry will be disease-free.

> ❝ *The choices many religious groups leave you with are either no sex at all or uneducated sex.* ❞

To most abstaining teens, marriage is the golden light at the end of the perilous tunnel of dating—despite what their parents' experience may have been. Though Amanda's mother and father have had a long and stable union, Karl Nicoletti separated from Chris's mother when Chris was in fifth grade. His fiancee moved in with Chris and Karl two years ago; Chris's mother now has a year-and-a-half-old son out of wedlock. Chris and Amanda talk about marriage in the abstract, but they want to go to college first, and they're looking at schools on opposite sides of the country. "I think we could stay together," Chris says. Amanda agrees. "Like we have complete trust in each other," she says. "It's just not hard for us." Whether the bond between them is strong enough to withstand a long-distance relationship is yet to be seen. For now, Chris and Amanda mostly look ahead to their next weekly ritual: the Tuesday pancake lunch.

The survivor

Remaining a virgin until marriage is neither an easy nor a common choice in Latoya Huggins's part of Paterson, N.J. At least three of her friends became single mothers while they were still in high school, one by an older man who now wants nothing to do with the child. "It's hard for her to finish school," Latoya says, "because she has to take the baby to get shots and stuff."

Latoya lives in a chaotic world: so far this year, more than a dozen people have been murdered in her neighborhood. It's a life that makes her sexuality seem like one of the few things she can actually control. "I don't even want a boyfriend until after college," says Latoya, who's studying to be a beautician at a technical high school. "Basically I want a lot out of life. My career choices are going to need a lot of time and effort."

Latoya, 18, could pass for a street-smart 28. She started thinking seriously about abstinence five years ago, when a national outreach program called Free Teens began teaching classes at her church. The classes reinforced what she already knew from growing up in Paterson—that discipline is the key to getting through your teen years alive. Earlier this year she dated a 21-year-old appliance salesman from her neighborhood, until Latoya heard that he was hoping she'd have sex with him. "We decided that we should just be friends," she explains, "before he cheated on me or we split up in a worse way."

> *Discipline is the key to getting through your teen years alive.*

So most days Latoya comes home from school alone. While she waits for her parents to return from work, she watches the Disney Channel or chills in her basement bedroom, which she's decorated with construction-paper cutouts of the names of her favorite pop stars, such as Nelly and Aaliyah. She feels safe there, she says, because "too many bad things are happening" outside. But bad things happen inside, too: last year she opened the door to a neighbor who forced his way inside and attempted to rape her. "He started trying to take my clothes off. I was screaming and yelling to the top of my lungs and nobody heard." Luckily, the phone rang. Latoya told the intruder it was her father, and that if she didn't answer he would come home right away. The man fled. Latoya tries not to think about what happened, although she feels "like dying" when she sees her attacker on the street. (Her parents decided not to press charges so she wouldn't have to testify in court.) Her goal is to graduate and get a job; she wants to stay focused and independent. "Boys make you feel like you're special and you're the only one they care about," she says. "A lot of girls feel like they need that. But my mother loves me and my father loves me, so there's no gap to fill."

The beauty queen

Even though she lives 700 miles from the nearest ocean, Daniela Aranda was recently voted Miss Hawaiian Tropic El

Paso, Texas, and her parents couldn't be prouder. They've displayed a picture of their bikini-clad daughter smack-dab in the middle of the living room. "People always say to me 'You don't look like a virgin'," says Daniela, 20, who wears supersparkly eye shadow, heavy lip liner and a low-cut black shirt. "But what does a virgin look like? Someone who wears white and likes to look at flowers?"

Daniela models at Harley-Davidson fashion shows, is a cheerleader for a local soccer team called the Patriots and hangs out with friends who work at Hooters. She's also an evangelical Christian who made a vow at 13 to remain a virgin, and she's kept that promise. "It can be done," she says. "I'm living proof." Daniela has never joined an abstinence program; her decision came from strong family values and deep spiritual convictions.

Daniela's arid East El Paso neighborhood, just a mile or so from the Mexican border, was built atop desert dunes, and the sand seems to be reclaiming its own by swallowing up back patios and sidewalks. The city, predominantly Hispanic, is home to the Fort Bliss Army base, breathtaking mesa views—and some of the highest teen-pregnancy rates in the nation. "There's a lot of girls that just want to get pregnant so they can get married and get out of here," Daniela says.

He's what you call a born-again virgin.

But she seems content to stay in El Paso. She studies business at El Paso Community College, dates a UTEP [University of Texas El Paso] football player named Mike and works as a sales associate at the A'gaci Too clothing store in the Cielo Vista Mall. She also tones at the gym and reads—especially books by the Christian author Joshua Harris. In "Boy Meets Girl," she's marked such passages as "Lust is never satisfied" with a pink highlighter. She's also saved an article on A.C. Green, the former NBA player who's become a spokesman for abstinence. "My boyfriend's coach gave it to him because the other guys sometimes say, 'Are you gay? What's wrong with you?' It's proof that if a famous man like Green can do it, so can he."

Daniela has been dating Mike for more than a year. He's had sex before, but has agreed to remain abstinent with her.

"He's what you call a born-again virgin," she says. "Or a secondary abstinent, or something like that. We just don't put ourselves in compromising situations. If we're together late at night, it's with my whole family."

Daniela knows about temptation: every time she walks out onstage in a bathing suit, men take notice. But she doesn't see a contradiction in her double life as virgin and beauty queen; rather, it's a personal challenge. "I did Hawaiian Tropic because I wanted to see if I could get into a bikini in front of all these people," she says. "I wasn't thinking, 'Oh, I'm going to win.' But I did, and I got a free trip to Houston's state finals. I met the owner of Hawaiian Tropic. It's like, wow, this is as good as it gets."

The ring bearer

Lenee Young is trying to write a paper for her Spanish class at Atlanta's Spelman College, but as usual she and her roommates can't help getting onto the subject of guys. "I love Ludacris," Lenee gushes. "I love everything about him. Morris Chestnut, too. He has a really pretty smile. Just gorgeous." But Lenee, 19, has never had a boyfriend, and has never even been kissed. "A lot of the guys in high school had already had sex," she says. "I knew that would come up, so I'd end all my relationships at the very beginning." Lenee decided back then to remain a virgin until marriage, and even now she feels little temptation to do what many of her peers are doing behind closed dormitory doors. "I feel that part of me hasn't been triggered yet," she says. "Sex is one of those things you can't miss until you have it."

> **" I don't feel like I've missed out. . . . I just feel like my time will come. "**

Last summer she went with a friend from her hometown of Pittsburgh to a Silver Ring Thing. These popular free events meld music videos, pyrotechnics and live teen comedy sketches with dire warnings about STDs. Attendees can buy a silver ring—and a Bible—for $12. Then, at the conclusion of the program, as techno music blares, they recite a pledge of abstinence and don their rings. "My friend, who's also a virgin, said I needed to go so I could get a ring," Lenee says. "It was fun, like the music and everything. And afterwards they had a dance and a bonfire."

The idea of abstinence was not new to Lenee. In high school she participated in a program sponsored by the University of Pittsburgh Medical Center called Postponing Sexual Involvement. Her mother had discussed it with her—once—the week before she left for college. Two of her closest friends are also virgins; the trio jokingly call themselves The Good Girls Club. But student life can sometimes be a shock to her sensibilities. "Another friend of mine and this guy were talking about how they didn't use a condom. He said, 'I like it raw.' I was like, 'Oh, my goodness'."

> **❝** *Physically, it did feel good, but emotionally, it felt really awkward. It was not what I expected it to be.* **❞**

And then there was the recent party that began with truth-or-dare questions. The first one: have you ever kissed a boy? Young was the only woman who said no, and everybody in the room was stunned. "Are you serious? We gotta find you a boyfriend!" But Lenee wasn't embarrassed. "I don't feel like I've missed out," she says. "I just feel like my time will come." Until then, she sports that shiny silver ring.

The renewed virgin

Lucian Schulte had always planned to wait until he was married to have sex, but that was before a warm night a couple of years ago when the green-eyed, lanky six-footer found himself with an unexpected opportunity. "She was all for it," says Lucian, now 18. "It was like, 'Hey, let's give this a try'." The big event was over in a hurry and lacked any sense of intimacy. "In movies, if people have sex, it's always romantic," he says. "Physically, it did feel good, but emotionally, it felt really awkward. It was not what I expected it to be."

While the fictional teens of "American Pie" would have been clumsily overjoyed, Lucian, raised Roman Catholic, was plagued by guilt. "I was worried that I'd given myself to someone and our relationship was now a lot more serious than it was before," he says. "It was like, 'Now, what is she going to expect from me?'" Lucian worried, too, about disease and pregnancy. He promised himself never again.

Lucian, now an engineering major at the University of Alberta in Canada, is a "renewed virgin." His parents are strong proponents of chastity, and he attended school-sponsored abstinence classes. But the messages didn't hit home until he'd actually had sex. "It's a pretty special thing, and it's also pretty serious," he says. "Abstinence has to do with 'Hey, are you going to respect this person?'" He has dated since his high-school affair, and is now hoping a particular cute coed from Edmonton will go out with him. "But I'll try to restrict myself to kissing," he says. "Not because I think everything else is bad. But the more you participate with someone, the harder it's going to be to stop."

It's not easy to practice such restraint, especially when those around him do not. Lucian lives in a single room, decorated with ski-lift tickets and a "Scooby-Doo" poster, in an all-male dorm, but he says most students "get hitched up, sleep around and never see each other again." Meanwhile he does his best to push his own sexual urges from his mind. "I try to forget about it, but I have to say it sucks. Homework is a good thing to do, and going out for a run usually works." He also goes to Sunday mass. Lucian figures he can hold out until he's married, which he hopes will be by the time he's 30. "I'm looking forward to an intimate experience with my wife, who I'll truly love and want to spend the rest of my life with," says Lucian. "It's kind of corny, but it's for real."

4

Teenage Virginity Pledges Are Not Working

Kaiser Family Foundation

The "Daily Reproductive Health Report" is an online publication produced by the Kaiser Family Foundation, a research institute specializing in the study of health care and health policy.

According to a federal study, 88 percent of the teenagers who pledged to remain virgins until marriage broke their vows. The study also found that the pledgers were less likely to get tested for STDs, raising the risk of infecting other people. Some argue that because they are likely to break their virginity pledges, teenagers must be taught how to practice safe sex. Proponents of the virginity pledge movement, on the other hand, say the study shows that educators must work harder to help pledgers keep their vows.

Teenagers who make "virginity pledges" to abstain from sexual intercourse until marriage have similar rates of sexually transmitted diseases as teens who have not committed to remain abstinent, according to a study presented . . . at the 2004 National STD Prevention Conference in Philadelphia, the AP/Long Island *Newsday* reports. Peter Bearman, sociology department chair at Columbia University, and Hannah Bruckner of Yale University, who co-authored the study, used data from the National Longitudinal Study of Adolescent Health, which is funded by the National Institute of Child Health and Human

Development and CDC [Centers for Disease Control and Prevention]. The study examined a nationally representative sample of 12,000 teenagers who entered the study when they were between the ages of 12 and 18. Researchers asked participants whether they had taken a virginity pledge and if they had engaged in sexual intercourse and tested them for three common STDs [sexually transmitted diseases]: chlamydia, gonorrhea and trichomoniasis, according to the *New York Times.*

Pledgers versus non-pledgers

Approximately 99% of teenagers who did not pledge abstinence until marriage had sex before marriage, according to the study. About 88% of participants who had pledged to remain virgins until marriage reported having sexual intercourse before marriage. However, teenagers who pledged to remain virgins had sexual intercourse an average of 18 months later than teens who did not take a pledge. In addition, by age 23, 50% of individuals who had made pledges as teenagers were married, compared with 25% of individuals who did not make a virginity pledge, according to the study. Among white teens who pledged virginity until marriage, 2.8% tested positive for an STD, compared with 3.5% of white teens who did not pledge. Black teens who pledged virginity had an STD rate of 18.1%, compared with 20.3% for black teens who did not pledge, and Hispanic teens who pledged to remain virgins had an STD rate of 6.7%, compared with 8.6% among Hispanic teens who did not pledge, according to the *AP/Newsday.* The differences between STD rates of pledgers and non-pledgers were not statistically significant, according to Bearman.

Pledgers are at risk

Bearman and Bruckner said that teenagers who pledged to remain virgins until marriage were less likely than other teens to have undergone STD testing and know their STD status, which could increase their risk of STD transmission to sexual partners, according to the *Times.* For male pledgers, 5.2% were tested for STDs, compared with 9.1% of non-pledgers; 14% of female teens who took a virginity pledge were tested for STDs, compared with 28% of teen girls who did not take a pledge. Also, virginity pledgers were "much less likely" to use contraception the first time they had sex, *Reuters* reports. Only 40% of male teenagers who took a pledge reported having used a condom in the past year, compared with 59% of those who did not take a virginity pledge, according to *Reuters*. For female teens, 47% of pledgers reported having used a condom in the previous year, compared with 55% of teens who did not pledge. Teens who pledged to remain virgins until marriage also averaged fewer sexual partners, according to *Reuters*.

> *Virginity pledgers were 'much less likely' to use contraception the first time they had sex.*

Bearman said that telling teens to "'just say no,' without understanding risk or how to protect oneself from risk, turns out to create greater risk." He added that he did not know if teens who broke their pledges "did so initially with their fiances or with others" because the data had not been analyzed yet, according to the *Times*. However, he added, "After they break their pledge, the gates are open, and they catch up." Bearman said, "These [virginity pledge] movements that are ignorant of social science research defeat the purpose they set out to solve." He also said, "It's difficult to simultaneously prepare for sex and say you're not going to have sex," adding, "It is the combination of hidden sex and unsafe sex that creates a world where people underestimate the risk of STDs."

Signing a pledge card is not enough

Dorothy Mann, executive director of the Family Planning Council, a reproductive health services group, said, "It's a tragedy if we withhold from these kids information about how not to get STDs or not to get pregnant." Sexuality Information and Education Council of the United States President and CEO Tamara Kreinin said, "This study clearly demonstrates that it is critical for us to provide all our young people with open, honest and medically accurate information to protect themselves against STDs." She added, "It is time for lawmakers, including President Bush, to stop using young people for political purposes and stand up for their health and futures." Pat Fagan, who researches family and cultural issues for the Heritage Foundation, said that the study's finding that the pledges delayed sex and led to fewer partners "shows the power of the pledges by themselves," adding, "It also shows that alone, a one-time pledge is not enough. Anyone connected with the abstinence movement would never say it's enough." Jimmy Hester, spokesperson for "True Love Waits," a campaign launched in 1993 by the Southern Baptist Convention to promote abstinence until marriage, said that the group had followed the study for seven years but had not heard the latest findings, according to the *Times*. He added that he was concerned about the results "because we're not following up on pledges well enough," saying, "Signing a pledge card does not mean you are magically protected" from STDs. Ronald Valdiserri, deputy director of the CDC's National Center for HIV, STD and TB Prevention, said, "The study is not the final answer," adding, "It points to the need for additional research in this area to identify effective interventions and to understand what makes them work."

5

The STD Rates for Teens Are Epidemic

Kim Best

Kim Best is a senior writer and editor for Family Health International in Research Triangle Park, North Carolina.

Adolescents in the United States and other nations are facing a growing epidemic of STDs. The highest rates of new HIV infections typically occur among teenagers, who are also at great risk for gonorrhea, chlamydia, and syphilis. Adolescents in developing countries run an especially high risk for STDs because they tend not to be well informed about sexual matters and are often physically coerced into sexual relations. However, even when they have knowledge about STDs, they often do not take precautions to prevent them because they underestimate their risk. In addition, even though they may understand that condoms could help prevent STDs, they are reluctant to buy them or do not use them correctly. Teenagers also often do not get the treatment they need for STDs because they do not know about the available services, cannot afford expensive tests and drugs, or are afraid to seek help. Their failure to get treatment can lead to serious and sometimes fatal conditions.

About a third of the world's 34 million HIV-positive people are between 10 and 24 years old. In most parts of the world, most new HIV infections are among adolescents, particularly among females. Notably, a substantial number of pregnant adolescents in sub-Saharan Africa are infected. Moreover, about a third of the 333 million new sexually transmitted disease (STD)

Kim Best, "Many Youth Face Grim STD Risks," *Family Health International Network*, vol. 20, 2000. Copyright © 2000 by Family Health International. For more information see www.fhi.org.

cases each year—excluding HIV—occur among people younger than 25, and recent data suggest that the adolescent STD epidemic is growing, adds Dr. Willard Cates, Jr., president of Family Health International (FHI) and an expert on STDs.

"Younger people are more likely to adopt and maintain safe sexual behaviors than are older people with well-established sexual habits, making youth excellent candidates for prevention efforts," says Dr. Cates. "Reducing adolescent infections will ultimately result in fewer infections among all age groups."

However, many interrelated and complex factors that put adolescents at risk of STDs will not be changed easily or quickly. In many settings, these include poor education, unemployment and poverty. Also, urbanization tends to disrupt family relationships, social networks and traditional mores, while generating more opportunity for sexual encounters.

> *Even when adolescents have accurate knowledge about STDs, they often do not heed warnings to reduce risky sexual behaviors.*

Adolescents in some places tend to delay their sexual debut, but others begin to have sex quite early. This is important because teenagers who have an early sexual debut are more likely to have sex with high-risk partners or multiple partners and are less likely to use barrier methods of contraception such as latex condoms, which offer STD protection.

In a 1999 analysis of studies of adolescent sexual risk-taking in several developing countries, sexual debut as early as nine years was reported in Zimbabwe. In Chile, a third of young people reported having had sex before age 15. In the analysis, today's young people in Cambodia were becoming sexually active at younger ages than in the past. And in Costa Rica and Colombia, a trend among youth to have a wider repertoire of practices (anal and oral sex) was noted.

Also putting both male and female adolescents at risk of STDs is their lack of information about sexual matters, as well as STD prevention, symptoms and treatment. Approximately one quarter of some 1,000 students surveyed in Karnataka, India, mistakenly thought that a vaccine and a cure for HIV infection existed, while half of 970 secondary-school students surveyed in Nigeria did not know that HIV causes AIDS. In a survey of more than 300 U.S. college students, the majority of students knew little about human papilloma virus (HPV) infection, transmission or prevalence, although HPV infection is the most common STD in this age group and the primary cause of cervical cancer.

Teens do not realize their risk is high

Even when adolescents have accurate knowledge about STDs, they often do not heed warnings to reduce risky sexual behaviors. Some adolescents at high risk, for example, do not adopt safer behaviors because they incorrectly perceive their risk as low.

Familiarity with a sexual partner often leads to a perception of decreased risk. In a study from Malawi, girls perceived little risk in having sexual relations with a boy whose mother knew their family. In U.S. studies, adolescents assumed that STD prevalence among their close friends was lower than among other teens and were surprised if they became infected by a close friend. In one U.S. study of some 200 college students, inconsistent condom use was strongly associated with the belief that sexual partners were uninfected with HIV or other STDs. These beliefs were based on individuals' perceptions that they "knew" their partner's sexual history or "just knew" their partner was safe. . . .

Perceived risk can also decrease as a relationship matures. While half of the 200 U.S. college students in this study reported consistent condom use in the first month of their sexual relationships, condom use decreased as relationships progressed.

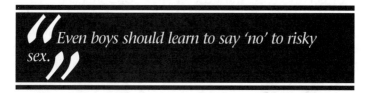

Even boys should learn to say 'no' to risky sex.

Also affecting perceived risk, says FHI's Dr. Cates, "is the tendency for adolescents in steady relationships to be more concerned about preventing pregnancy than the risk of contracting an STD. As oral contraception use increases, condom use decreases. However, dual protection against both STDs and pregnancy is best achieved by using both male condoms and effective female contraceptive methods."

Other adolescents at high risk may not adopt safer behaviors simply because they are passing through a stage of life in which risk-taking is particularly attractive. Many adolescents either feel they have nothing to lose or feel they are invulnerable and cannot lose. Others are strongly influenced by peers. As one respondent in a field study conducted in Kenya commented: "The youngsters of the new generation really look at sex like it is an 'in thing.' You know it is 'macho' now to go to bed with a woman. Even if it is going out for a social drink, you end up in the bedroom. The bottom line is that you will have sex."

The problem of getting condoms

To avoid acquiring STDs, adolescents need to have the skills and self-confidence to either abstain from sexual relations or to use condoms consistently and correctly.

"Even boys should learn to say 'no' to risky sex," wrote Fred Otimgu, a student at St. Joseph's College in Layibi, Uganda, in a recent issue of *Straight Talk*, a newspaper for students that encourages youth to wait to have sexual relations or to use condoms. "When I suggested to my girlfriend that we use a condom and she refused, I left her because of my fear of HIV/STDs."

> *Adolescent girls are . . . infected with HIV more often than are adolescent boys.*

Correct and consistent use of latex condoms is the most effective means of preventing STD infection among sexually active people who are at risk. In many settings, condom use among adolescents has been increasing. However, adolescents may have difficulty obtaining condoms and knowing how to use them correctly.

Most 16- to 22-year-old participants in focus group discussions held in South Africa as part of a commercial marketing initiative said they did not use condoms due to lack of availability. Most of the 78 participants simply did not have the courage to ask for condoms at pharmacies and clinics. "Many said they were tired of being told that they should not be having sex or being refused condoms because the person who is supposed to be distributing them imposed their morality on the youth," says an HIV-positive man who helped conduct the focus groups.

For this reason, he said in an interview, "condoms need to be available wherever youth gather or 'hang out.' Also, most participants reported that they would prefer to purchase their condoms from their peers or younger sales people—not someone who is old enough to be their parent. They would also prefer to get condoms from vending machines in such places as game arcades, public toilets, night clubs, music shops or Internet cafes."

Inexperience with condoms is another problem. Often unfamiliar with condoms and apt to engage in spontaneous sex, adolescents may have problems anticipating intercourse and putting on the condom in a timely manner. Peer-group pressure plays a role, either facilitating or inhibiting condom use. "Issues of image seemed to outweigh risks," says the HIV-positive man who helped conduct the South African focus groups. "If obtaining or using condoms was too embarrassing, boring or silly, they would prefer not to use them."

Girls are more vulnerable to STD infection

In developing countries, up to 60 percent of new HIV infections are among 15- to 24-year-olds, with generally twice as many new infections in young women than young men. Recent studies in several African populations indicate that 15- to 19-year-old girls are five or six times more likely to be HIV-positive than boys their own age. In one area of Kenya, 22 percent of 15- to 19-year-old girls in the general population were HIV-infected, compared with just 4 percent of boys of the same age.

Similarly, the reported incidence of syphilis, gonorrhea and particularly chlamydia has been generally higher among female teenagers than among males the same age throughout 16 developed countries (the United States, Canada, and 14 in Europe). For developing countries, very little age- or sex-specific data are available for STDs other than HIV.

Why are young women more vulnerable than young men—or older women—to STD infection? In the adolescent female, a specific type of cell lining the inside of the cervical canal extends onto the outer surface of the cervix, where exposure to sexually transmitted pathogens is greater. These cells are more vulnerable to infections such as chlamydia and gonorrhea. As women age, this vulnerable tissue recedes and usually no longer extends onto the outer surface of the cervix.

Adolescent girls are also infected with HIV more often than

are adolescent boys because many have sex with older men, who are more likely to be infected than adolescent men. Older men are more likely than younger men to be able to give gifts, money or favors. . . . Also, surveys show that young women are less likely than males of the same age to report condom use.

The risks for young males

Young male adolescents also face risks. In developing countries, older men, family members or peers often encouraged young men to begin having sex, often with potentially high-risk partners: sex workers, other men or older women. In Uganda, older women appear to seek younger boys for sexual favors and, in Malawi, younger boys seek older women. In Mexico, Guatemala and Jamaica, most of young males' first sexual relationships have been reported to be with older women. In Mumbai, India, research indicated that older married women are sexual partners of some young male adolescents from the neighborhood. In addition, some young boys have sex with men. Often, relations involve unprotected anal sex, which can cause abrasions and cuts through which HIV can pass into the receptive partner's bloodstream.

In-depth interviews in Karachi, Pakistan, by a group promoting sexual health, called Aahung (an Urdu word meaning "harmony"), suggest that adolescent boys from low-income communities are at least as vulnerable to STDs as are girls. "Boys have much more freedom to experiment," said Shazia Premjee of Aahung in an interview.

> *Delay or lack of treatment of STDs can have serious, even fatal, consequences.*

"Boys also have more access to information about sex," she says, "much of which is filled with myths and misconceptions that lead to unhealthy behaviors. Unlike girls—who generally are not allowed to leave the home unaccompanied after puberty and receive guidance from older, female members of the family—boys do not talk about sexual health with adults in their households. Sexual misconceptions, therefore, are not corrected. Also, many of the boys we interviewed had had various sexual experiences with members of the same sex."

Both young men and women sell sex. But, unlike male adolescents who often become prostitutes voluntarily, girls usually do so against their wishes. In Thailand, young girls most commonly sell sex because their parents urgently need money. Young sex workers are at a higher risk of acquiring an STD than older prostitutes because they have less power to negotiate condom use with partners. The consequences can be grim. In Cambodia, for example, nearly a third of sex workers ages 13 to 19 years are infected with HIV.

Meanwhile, a substantial number of girls have sexual relations because they are physically coerced: In various populations, between a quarter and a third of young women report having experienced coerced sexual relations. The plight of the world's 100 million street children—most of whom are between 11 and 14 years old and live in the large cities of developing countries—is even more bleak. In Guatemala, 95 percent of street girls had experienced sexual abuse. In Brazil, street youth are considered to be at high risk of HIV or STDs in part because of very early sexual debut, frequently the result of coercion.

> *Up to one in every three pregnant adolescents in some settings is HIV-infected.*

Anal intercourse presents the greatest risk of sexual HIV transmission. However, in numerous studies, heterosexuals have been found to use condoms less often for anal sex than for vaginal sex. Furthermore, a study among 800 sexually active New York City adolescents ages 13 to 21 years showed that females practicing anal sex (about 14 percent of the 483 women in the study) were less likely to use condoms with a non-steady—and potentially more risky—partner. Of young women who practiced anal intercourse, 84 percent never used condoms with steady partners, but even more—96 percent—never used condoms with casual partners.

STD complications

STD treatment for adolescents is often inadequate for a variety of reasons, including the fact that many adolescents do not know about available services. Services may also be inaccessible because clinics are far away or have limited hours; tests and drugs may be too expensive, female adolescents may fear pelvic examinations (even though such exams may not be necessary), young people may be too embarrassed or feel too guilty to seek treatment, and health providers may be reluctant to serve adolescents. Health facilities in places as diverse as Antigua, Senegal and Thailand have been found to deny adolescents privacy and confidentiality, and staff have been rude in some places. . . .

Correct diagnosis and treatment of STDs is particularly challenging among young women, since such STDs as gonorrhea and chlamydia are often asymptomatic. Female adolescents with symptoms tend to delay seeking help, compared with older women.

Delay or lack of treatment of STDs can have serious, even fatal, consequences. Untreated STDs—particularly chlamydia and gonorrhea—can cause pelvic inflammatory disease (PID) throughout the upper genital tract. Inflammation and scarring from this infection can either block the fallopian tubes or damage the tubal lining. Long-term consequences include chronic pain, tubal infertility or life-threatening ectopic pregnancy.

Not only is PID more common among sexually active female adolescents than older sexually active women, but female adolescents are more likely to be infected again and to experience a recurrence of PID. This is because, by beginning sexual activity early, they have more time to be infected. Repeated infections increase the risk of infertility. . . .

If an STD-infected adolescent becomes pregnant, the disease can be transmitted to her fetus or infant. Bacterial vaginosis and trichomoniasis are related to preterm delivery and low-birthweight infants.

The following STDs can cause a variety of diseases in infants—gonorrhea can cause conjunctivitis, sepsis and meningitis; chlamydia can cause conjunctivitis, pneumonia, bronchiolitis and otitis media; syphilis can result in congenital syphilis and neonatal death; hepatitis B can cause hepatitis and cirrhosis; herpes simplex virus can cause disseminated, central nervous system and localized lesions; and human papilloma virus can cause laryngeal papillomatosis. HIV can cause pediatric AIDS. Up to one in every three pregnant adolescents in some settings is HIV-infected.

6

Teens' Sexual Activity Can Lead to Depression and Suicide Attempts

Robert E. Rector, Kirk A. Johnson, and Lauren R. Noyes

Robert E. Rector is senior research fellow, Kirk A. Johnson is senior policy analyst, and Lauren R. Noyes is director of research projects in domestic policy at the Heritage Foundation. The Heritage Foundation is a research and educational institute.

A study by the Heritage Foundation's Center for Data Analysis reveals a link between teenage sexual activity and emotional health. Sexually active teenagers are more likely to suffer from depression and feelings of worthlessness than sexually inactive teenagers. In addition, sexually active teenagers attempt suicide at much higher rates than abstinent teenagers. The fact that a majority of teenagers express regrets about being sexually active suggests that the cause of their emotional stress is their sexual activity. Teenagers should therefore be taught that sexual activity is likely to lead to depression.

Teenage sexual activity is an issue of widespread national concern. Although teen sexual activity has declined in recent years, the overall rate is still high. In 1997, approximately 48 percent of American teenagers of high-school age were or had been sexually active.

The problems associated with teen sexual activity are well-known. Every day, 8,000 teenagers in the United States become infected by a sexually transmitted disease. This year [2003], nearly 3 million teens will become infected. Overall, roughly one-quarter of the nation's sexually active teens have been infected by a sexually transmitted disease (STD).

Teen sexual activity affects emotional well-being

The problems of pregnancy and out-of-wedlock childbearing are also severe. In 2000, some 240,000 children were born to girls aged 18 or younger. Nearly all these teenage mothers were unmarried. These mothers and their children have an extremely high probability of long-term poverty and welfare dependence. Less widely known are the psychological and emotional problems associated with teenage sexual activity. The present study examines the linkage between teenage sexual activity and emotional health. The findings show that:

> When compared to teens who are not sexually active, teenage boys and girls who are sexually active are significantly less likely to be happy and more likely to feel depressed.

> When compared to teens who are not sexually active, teenage boys and girls who are sexually active are significantly more likely to attempt suicide.

Thus, in addition to its role in promoting teen pregnancy and the current epidemic of STDs, early sexual activity is a substantial factor in undermining the emotional well-being of American teenagers.

A nationwide survey

The data used in this analysis are taken from the National Longitudinal Survey of Adolescent Health, Wave II, 1996. This "Ad-Health" survey is a nationwide survey designed to examine the health-related behaviors of adolescents in middle school and high school. Its public-use database contains responses from approximately 6,500 adolescents, representative of teenagers across the nation. The survey is funded by the National Institute of Child Health and Human Development (NICHD) and 17 other federal agencies.

This Heritage CDA [Center for Data Analysis] analysis focuses on the link between sexual activity and emotional well-being among teens in high school years (ages 14 through 17). The Ad-Health survey asks students whether they have "ever had sexual intercourse." For purposes of analysis, teens who answered yes to this question are labeled as "sexually active" and those who answered no are labeled as "not sexually active."

The survey also records the emotional health of teens. Students are asked how often, in the past week, they "felt depressed." They are provided with four possible answers to the question: They felt depressed
(a) Never or rarely,
(b) Sometimes,
(c) A lot of the time, or
(d) Most of the time or all of the time.

For purposes of analysis, the classification of depressed is given to those teens who answered yes to options "c" or "d"— that is, they said they felt depressed a lot, most, or all of the time. Thus, throughout the paper, the terms "depressed" or "depression" refer to this general state of continuing unhappiness rather than to a more specific sense of clinical depression.

Sexual activity and depression

The Ad-Health data reveal substantial differences in emotional health between those teens who are sexually active and those who are not. . . .

> A full quarter (25.3 percent) of teenage girls who are sexually active report that they are depressed all, most, or a lot of the time. By contrast, only 7.7 percent of teenage girls who are not sexually active report that they are depressed all, most, or a lot of the time. Thus, sexually active girls are more than three times more likely to be depressed than are girls who are not sexually active.
>
> Some 8.3 percent of teenage boys who are sexually active report that they are depressed all, most, or a lot of the time. By contrast, only 3.4 percent of teenage boys who are not sexually active are depressed all, most, or a lot of the time. Thus, boys who are sexually active are more than twice as likely to be depressed as are those who are not sexually active. . . .

The link between teen sexual activity and depression is supported by clinical experience. Doctor of adolescent medicine Meg Meeker writes, "Teenage sexual activity routinely leads to emotional turmoil and psychological distress. . . . [Sexual permissiveness leads] to empty relationships, to feelings of self-contempt and worthlessness. All, of course, precursors to depression."

Sexual activity and attempted suicide

The Ad-Health survey also asks students whether they have attempted suicide during the past year. . . . The link between sexual activity and attempted suicide is clear.

> *Early sexual activity is a substantial factor in undermining the emotional well-being of American teenagers.*

A full 14.3 percent of girls who are sexually active report having attempted suicide. By contrast, only 5.1 percent of sexually inactive girls have attempted suicide. Thus, sexually active girls are nearly three times more likely to attempt suicide than are girls who are not sexually active.

Among boys, 6.0 percent of those who are sexually active have attempted suicide. By contrast, only 0.7 percent of boys who are not sexually active have attempted suicide. Thus, sexually active teenage boys are eight times more likely to attempt suicide than are boys who are not sexually active.

Social background factors

The differences in emotional health between sexually active and inactive teens are clear. However, it is possible that the differences in emotional well-being might be driven by social background factors rather than sexual activity *per se*. For example, if students of lower socioeconomic status are more likely to be sexually active, the greater frequency of depression among those teens might be caused by socioeconomic status rather than sexual activity.

To account for that possibility, additional analysis was per-

formed in which race, gender, exact age, and family income
were entered as control variables. This means that each teen
was compared to other teens who were identical in gender, age,
race, and income.

The introduction of these control or background variables
had virtually no effect on the correlations between sexual activity and depression and suicide. In simple terms, when teens were
compared to other teens who were identical in gender, race, age
and family income, those who were sexually active were significantly more likely to be depressed and to attempt suicide than
were those who were not sexually active.

Teens express regrets over sexual activity

The significantly lower levels of happiness and higher levels of
depression among sexually active teens suggest that sexual activity leads to a decrease in happiness and well-being among
many, if not most, teenagers. This conclusion is corroborated
by the fact that the majority of sexually active teens express
reservations and concerns about their personal sexual activity.

> *Teenage sexual activity routinely leads to emotional turmoil and psychological distress.*

For example, a recent [2000] poll by the National Campaign to Prevent Teen Pregnancy asked the question, "If you
have had sexual intercourse, do you wish you had waited
longer?" Among those teens who reported that they had engaged in intercourse, nearly two-thirds stated that they wished
they had waited longer before becoming sexually active. By
contrast, only one-third of sexually active teens asserted that
their commencement of sexual activity was appropriate and
that they did not wish they had waited until they were older.
Thus, among sexually active teens, those who regretted early
sexual activity outnumbered those without such concerns by
nearly two to one. . . .

Concerns and regrets about sexual activity are strongest
among teenage girls. Almost three-quarters of sexually active
teen girls admit they wish they had delayed sexual activity until they were older. Among sexually active teenage girls, those

with regrets concerning their initial sexual activity outnumbered those without regrets by nearly three to one.

> *❝The majority of sexually active teens express reservations and concerns about their personal sexual activity.❞*

The dissatisfaction and regrets expressed by teenagers concerning their own sexual activity is striking. Overall, a majority of sexually active boys and nearly three-quarters of sexually active girls regard their own initial sexual experience unfavorably—as an event they wish they had avoided.

Early sexual activity reduces teen happiness

While the association between teen sexual activity and depression is clear, that association may be subject to different theoretical interpretations. For example, it might be that depressed teenagers turn to sexual activity in an effort to assuage or escape their depression. In this interpretation, the link between sexual activity and depression might be caused by a higher level of sexual activity among those who are already depressed before commencing sexual activity. Thus, depression might lead to greater sexual activity rather than sexual activity's leading to depression.

In limited cases, this explanation may be correct; some depressed teens may experiment with sexual activity in an effort to escape their depression. However, as a general interpretation of the linkage between depression and teen sexual activity, this reasoning seems inadequate for two reasons. First, . . . the differences in happiness and depression between sexually active and inactive teens are widespread and are not the result of a small number of depressed individuals. This is especially true for girls. Second, the fact that a majority of teens express regrets concerning their own initial sexual activity strongly suggests that such activity leads to distress and emotional turmoil among many, if not most, teens.

Hence, the most likely explanation of the overall link between teen sexual activity and depression is that early sexual activity leads to emotional stress and reduces teen happiness.

Moreover, theoretical questions about whether teen sexual activity leads to depression or, conversely, whether depression leads to teen sexual activity should not distract attention from the clear message that adult society should be sending to teens. Teens should be told that sexual activity in teen years is clearly linked to reduced personal happiness. Teens who are depressed should be informed that sexual activity is likely to exacerbate, rather than alleviate, their depression. Teens who are not depressed should be told that sexual activity in teen years is likely to substantially reduce their happiness and personal well-being.

The dangers of teenage sexual activity

Sexual activity among teenagers is the major driving factor behind the well-publicized problems of the high incidence of teenage STDs and teen pregnancy. The analysis presented in this paper also shows that sexual activity is directly connected to substantial problems among teens regarding emotional health.

Teenagers of both genders who are sexually active are substantially less likely to be happy and more likely to be depressed than are teenagers who are not sexually active.

Teenagers of both genders who are sexually active are substantially more likely to attempt suicide than are teenagers who are not sexually active.

7

Homosexual Activist Groups Are Recruiting Students into Homosexuality

Ed Vitagliano

Ed Vitagliano is the news editor of the AFA Journal, *a monthly publication of the American Family Association. The American Family Association is a nonprofit organization that promotes family values.*

Homosexual activists use the nation's public school system to encourage students to experiment with homosexuality at a time when they are most confused about their sexual orientation. Various clubs and organizations that were formed to protect and support homosexual teens actually encourage young people to participate in homosexual activity. This experimentation is dangerous because people whose first experience of sex is homosexual are likely to engage in homosexual behavior as adults. Parents should be worried about homosexual activists because they are trying to recruit curious teens to accept a homosexual lifestyle.

What is the effect on children and teenagers when they are surrounded by a message that not only defends homosexuality as normal, natural and healthy, but recommends it as a sexual taste? Are young people being recruited into the homosexual lifestyle?

Ed Vitagliano, "Targeting Children, Part Three: Activists Encouraging Experimentation," www.afa.net, May 2001. Copyright © 2001 by the American Family Association. Reproduced by permission.

Confusing impressionable minds

Even in the best of times, young people very often find themselves confused about many issues—not the least of which is sex. Whether it is part of the normal adolescent journey to sexual identity or a spin-off effect of the current debate over homosexuality, some young people do question whether or not they are heterosexual.

For example, in a 1992 survey of nearly 35,000 Minnesota youth (grades 7 through 12), homosexual researcher Gary Remafedi at the University of Minnesota found that 25.9% of 12-year-olds were not sure whether they were heterosexual or homosexual.

But Ramafedi also found that such confusion begins to decrease as students grow older. Research by Dr. Kirk Cameron concurred. In a paper published in 1995 by Family Research Institute (FRI), that study found that while 25% of kids were unsure of their sexual orientation at age 12, that percentage steadily declined to about 5% by age 18.

Obviously, this early period of confusion is a critical time for young people. But the resulting confusion created *by* homosexuals *about* sexual orientation adds to the sexual confusion of young people. And even more insidious is the manner in which homosexual activists take advantage of this confusion by enthusiastically encouraging young people to *experiment* with homosexuality.

In Northboro, Massachusetts, for example, parents of freshman students were stunned to discover that their kids had been invited by their high school history teacher to try homosexuality. History teacher Douglas Matthews—an advisor to the school's "gay-straight" student alliance—handed out a questionnaire that asked, "If you've never slept with a person of the same sex and enjoyed it, is it possible that all you need is a good gay lover?"

Homosexual activists take advantage of schools

It may shock parents to learn that the nation's public school system is being used by homosexual activists as a conduit, herding confused children into the homosexual community. Under the guise of protecting homosexual teens, young people are given unrestricted access to homosexual groups. Once channeled there, however, there is no limit to the depths of same-sex debauchery to which teens may be exposed.

In Seattle, for example, the "Sexual Minority Advocacy Council" (SMAC) was created "to help ensure that [the Seattle public schools] are providing a safe environment for everyone who learns, works or interacts . . ." according to school superintendent John H. Stanford.

But with the student-safety concern out in front, the purpose of SMAC then "bleeds over" into other areas. A SMAC pamphlet produced by the Seattle Education Association and made available to all students, included a list of resources that amounts to a Seatlle same-sex smorgasbord for curious teens, complete with phone numbers: Seattle Counseling Services for Sexual Minorities; Lesbian Resource Center; Gay, Lesbian, Bisexual Transgender Youth Information Line; Lambert House Gay, Lesbian, Bisexual and Transgender Youth Drop-In Center; Parents, Families and Friends of Lesbians and Gays (PFLAG); and Gay/Lesbian Straight Education Network (GLSEN).

> **❝** *Young people very often find themselves confused about many issues—not the least of which is sex.* **❞**

What do kids find when they access the homosexual activist groups provided as resources by the pamphlet? When Eleanor Durham of Parents and Teachers for Responsible Schools checked the GLSEN website, for example, she was shocked by what she found. GLSEN's home page was an Internet doorway into every sort of pro-homosexual venue imaginable.

One GLSEN link, for example, was to a website that welcomed young people "who are searching out their sexual orientation." It asked young visitors, "Do you feel that you *might be* bisexual, gay, or lesbian? This is the place for you." (Emphasis added.) . . .

Thus young people, who may truly be confused about their sexuality or simply curious, are literally "funneled" from schools through supposedly protective activist groups into the world of the homosexual lifestyle. And once there, susceptible children can be lured into homosexual pornography, same-sex friendships and, ultimately, participation in homosexual activity.

While radical gay activists insist that a pro-homosexual curriculum in schools does not increase homosexual experimentation, experience proves otherwise.

One study published in 1998 of almost 2,000 high school students in the Los Angeles area focused on the relationship between condom availability and increased sexual activity. The study was conducted by UCLA and published by the Alan Guttmacher Institute in *Family Planning Perspectives.*

One of the most overlooked results of the study, according to FRI, was a shocker: *homosexual experimentation among the teens doubled following safe sex instruction.* And of equal concern to FRI was the finding that 40% of *heterosexual* kids in the study had tried anal sex with their partners—a practice that significantly increases the risk of disease for the participants. . . .

Homosexual adults initiate adolescents

But experimentation among teens and their peers is not the only concern for parents. Teens confused about their sexuality often consummate their first same-sex experience with an older homosexual, and statistics demonstrate that such first sexual experiences are a powerful force for molding sexual identity.

Journalist David Lipsky spent nine months traveling the U.S. and interviewing homosexual teenagers about their lifestyles, culminating in an article written for *Rolling Stone.* Although the tone of Lipsky's article was sympathetic to homosexual youth, one of the things he found was a fluid interaction between homosexuals of different ages. . . .

> *Young people, who may truly be confused about their sexuality or simply curious, are literally 'funneled' from schools . . . into the world of the homosexual lifestyle.*

From the homosexual teens who frequented one Atlanta mall, Lipsky learned that a lot of the young men had their first sexual experiences with an older man. Shannon Curtis, for example, had his homosexual initiation with two adult homosexual coworkers when they invited the then 14-year-old Curtis to their apartment.

Statistically this intergenerational sexual interaction is not an aberration. The SIGMA Project (1992), which interviewed and followed almost a thousand homosexuals in Britain over a three-year period, found that 50% of homosexuals had had their first same-sex experience with an adult by the age of 14. According to FRI, which reviewed the SIGMA data, 25% of those homosexuals had had sex with an adult by the age of 12 and 10% by the age of 10.

This adult homosexual fascination with younger partners is admitted even by the homosexual community. Two homosexual researchers (K. Jay and A. Young, 1979) found that 73% of male homosexuals had had sex *as adults* with boys 19 years old or younger—23% admitted to having sex with youth less than 16 years of age.

Other researchers (Bell, Weinberg and Hammersmith, 1978) found the same thing: a quarter of homosexuals admitted to having sex *as adults* with children and underaged teens.

> *A lot of the young men had their first sexual experiences with an older man.*

According to FRI head Dr. Paul Cameron, even in the controversial Kinsey research from the 1940s, which formed the basis of the Sexual Revolution and its progeny, the homosexual movement, homosexuals admitted a propensity for sex with minors. Kinsey found that 37% of homosexual adult men said they had had sex with youths under age 17, and 28% admitted to sexual relations with those under age 16.

Cameron also said that later research by the Kinsey Institute found in 1970 that 25% of homosexual men in San Francisco "admitted to having sex with boys aged 16 or younger while they themselves were at least 21."

Sadly, these early homosexual experiences play a significant role in locking a young person into the homosexual lifestyle. Researchers at the Kinsey Institute have found "a strong relationship between those whose first experience was homosexual and those who practised homosexuality later in life." The work of Bell, Weinberg and Hammersmith also found early homosexual experiences to be "very strong indicators of future, adult homosexuality."

The results of a 1983 study by FRI parallels this data. Researchers (P. Cameron, K. Cameron and K. Proctor) found that "two-thirds of the boys whose first experience was homosexual engaged in homosexual behavior as adults."

Is recruitment really occurring?

While regularly ridiculed by most pro-homosexual activists, the view that young people can be "recruited" into homosexuality, is accepted even by some homosexuals themselves.

Lesbian author and activist Donna Minkowitz, in a 1992 article entitled "Recruit, Recruit, Recruit!," recommended that homosexuals forget trying to convince society that people are homosexual by "nature."

"[I]t's time for us to abandon this defensive posture and walk upright on Earth. Maybe you didn't choose to be gay—that's fine. But I did," she said in *The Advocate*, a magazine catering to the homosexual community.

Activist Darrell Yates Rist, a co-founder of the Gay & Lesbian Alliance Against Defamation and a prominent homosexual author, said he believes it is certainly possible for children to be "lured by queer ideas" into the homosexual lifestyle.

Rist said this truth is understood intuitively by parents and worries them, because "they too understand that sexually free ideas are infectious and that, once introduced to the suggestion of same-sex love, their kids might just try it and like it."

8

Gay-Straight Alliances Provide Students with a Valuable Forum

Leslie Bulion

Leslie Bulion writes for Education World, an Internet resource for educators.

A gay-straight alliance (GSA) is a club for students who are concerned about creating a safe and accepting school environment. Federal law protects the rights of students to form GSAs. These clubs do not promote homosexuality; rather, they provide a safe forum for sexual-minority students to discuss the discrimination they often face in schools. Communities and administrators sometimes oppose GSAs, usually because they have misconceptions about the purpose of GSAs.

"Our school community was reluctant about the Gay-Straight Alliance (GSA) at first," Coginchaug (Connecticut) Regional High School teacher Liz Welsh told Education World. "There was concern about whether it could be in school and whether it was a legitimate extracurricular club."

"There is a lot of fear," added Candy Brickley, Welsh's colleague and GSA co-adviser in the small rural high school. "Some of the opposition comes from a concern that the club is a vehicle for recruitment into homosexuality."

"The opposition to our GSA believes that we are teaching kids how to be homosexual and promoting immorality," concurred Susan Meara, North Olmsted (Ohio) High School GSA community adviser.

"It's a way to get gay curriculum in schools," Tim Wild-mon, vice president of the Mississippi-based American Family Association, a national conservative watchdog group, was quoted as saying in the *Seattle Times* (October 16, 2000). "We view these kinds of clubs as an advancement of the homosex-ual cause."

A storm of controversy

Although there are more than 700 Gay-Straight Alliance ex-tracurricular clubs in the nation's schools, the existence of the clubs and their real or perceived agendas continue to ignite protest and controversy. Across the country, schools grapple with an issue that polarizes communities, setting religious and moral convictions against an educational mission to promote tolerance and diversity and provide support to all students. . . .

Constitutional protections

The rights of students to form GSAs are protected under federal law, according to Defending Gay/Straight Alliances and Other Gay-Related Groups in Public Schools Under the Equal Access Act, a memo of the Lambda Legal Defense and Education Fund. Any public high school that provides a meeting place during non-instructional time for even one voluntary, student-run, non-curricular club is providing a "limited open forum." Such a school is legally bound under the Federal Equal Access Act of 1984 to provide the same facilities to any extracurricular club, regardless of content. The First Amendment to the Constitu-tion protects the right of students to discuss what they choose, even if their views are in the minority.

> *The opposition to our GSA believes that we are teaching kids how to be homosexual and promoting immorality.*

According to an article in the *Denver Post*, on February 5, 1999, Jay Engeln, principal of Palmer High School, denied a re-quest to form a GSA. He expressed concern in the article that if he recognized the GSA, "he would also have to recognize devil worshipers, white supremacists, and hate groups" who could potentially request to meet on campus under the same legal protection.

"More than 700 Gay-Straight Alliances have formed in schools around the country over the past five years. I have yet to hear of any neo-Nazi hate clubs, so if they pop up now, I'll suspect outside groups are behind it," David S. Buckel, senior staff attorney for Lambda Legal Defense and Education Fund told Education World. "Keep in mind that schools always retain their authority to prohibit groups that materially and substantially interfere with the orderly conduct of educational activities within the school."

> *At least they know there is a safe place; someone is acknowledging them and the issues they face.*

According to Buckel's question-and-answer memo Defending Gay/Straight Alliances and Other Gay-Related Groups in Public Schools Under the Equal Access Act, if a group's *opponents* interfere with the orderly conduct of educational activities, a group cannot, by this "heckler's veto," be prevented from meeting.

GSAs promote student safety

Statistics make a sad but eloquent case for school support and intervention for students who belong to sexual minorities. In a 1999 survey of 496 sexual-minority students from 32 states, Youth Speak: GLSEN's School Climate Survey, more than 90 percent sometimes or frequently heard homophobic remarks. More than a third of those students heard homophobic remarks from *teachers*. Two-thirds of the students experienced verbal or physical harassment at school. The Massachusetts Board of Education 1999 Massachusetts Youth Risk Behavior Survey found that sexual-minority students are at significantly increased risk for violence. They are three times more likely to be the victims of weapon attacks at school and four times more likely to attempt suicide.

"I have seen changes in students who come to the GSA," teacher Welsh told Education World. "Kids with support move away from risk behaviors and experience school success. You can't pretend these kids don't exist. Even kids who won't step foot in the room benefit. At least they know there is a safe place; someone is acknowledging them and the issues they face."

> **"** *When any one of us is demeaned, we are all diminished.* **"**

"It is important to promote the psychological and physical health and intellectual development of *all* students," Dr. Arthur Lipkin of Harvard's Graduate School of Education and author of *Understanding Homosexuality, Changing Schools* told Education World. "We can reduce bigotry, self-hatred, and violence by increasing tolerance for sexuality differences." According to Lipkin, forming a GSA is one of the most important things a school can do to become a better, safer place for sexual-minority students.

Gay-straight alliance activities

From rural to urban settings, from east coast to west, GSAs around the country provide students with support and positive role models. The clubs channel teen energies from combating isolation to promoting education and increasing understanding.

"The Trinity (New York City) School GSA holds lunch meetings and sees films after school," teacher-adviser David Murphy told Education World. "We visit art galleries and attend national and local conferences. The students present workshops at those conferences and prepare school assembly programming."

"Spectrum [the North Olmsted Ohio GSA] meets three times per month at our off-campus location and once a month at school," said adviser Meara. "We have group discussions about confronting homophobia respectfully, and we host educational speakers. We lobbied the school board to amend the anti-harassment and anti-discrimination policies to include sexual orientation [with partial success]. We have organized observances of events such as National Coming Out Day, Day of Silence [a nationally organized show of solidarity with gay youth who can not speak out], and UN World AIDS Day."

"Our group is a true gay-straight alliance," Connecticut teacher-adviser Welsh told Education World. "The kids got organized and set goals so the group would not be just a gripe session. They sent speakers to health classes in our school. They have tried, with some community opposition, to participate in a panel at Diversity Day and to organize a Day of Silence." Welsh sighed. "Some students [not in the group] were irate. It is just a lack of understanding of what kids are facing."

Making schools safe, one meeting at a time

It is important to note that in these times of heightened fear about general school safety, sexual-minority harassment issues play a role in a dramatically disproportionate percentage of violent school incidents—for both gay *and* straight students.

"Homophobic conditioning compromises the integrity of people by pressuring them to treat others badly, contrary to basic humanity," said author [Dr. Warren] Blumenfeld, a University of Massachusetts (Amherst) professor of social justice education. "It compromises the entire school environment for all students and staff. When any one of us is demeaned, we are all diminished. When any group of people is scapegoated, it is ultimately everyone's concern."

Gay-Straight Alliances continue to spring up around the nation, meeting needs and serving a purpose in school communities—gay *and* straight. The most effective and efficient system of chipping away at fears and misperceptions may be one meeting at a time.

At Trinity School in Manhattan, teacher David Murphy has seen initial fears of the GSA as a "dating service" or "recruitment club" being addressed through the open-door meeting and activity policy. "The more you leave the doors open, the more you desensitize language such as *gay* by its casual, offhand use, the more you create an environment for kids to trust one another, and the easier everyone breathes. My strategy for institutional change is that of John Wayne on acting," Murphy joked. "Like he said, 'I show up, and I try not to knock over the furniture.'"

9
Television Educates Teens About Sexual Issues

Kate Langrall-Folb

Kate Langrall-Folb is director of the Media Project, a partnership of Advocates for Youth and the Kaiser Family Foundation. The Media Project provides research and information on sexual health to the entertainment industry.

Many schools and parents do not teach their children about sex. As a result, many teenagers look to television for answers to their questions. In fact, television can be a useful source of information about sex. Shows that include thoughtful themes about safe sex and AIDS influence teens and may be partly responsible for the drop in teen pregnancies. It is recommended that parents watch television programs about sexual issues with their children and have discussions about their concerns.

Editor's Note: The following selection is an interview with Kate Langrall-Folb that was broadcast on WebMD.

WebMD: *What is "responsible" and "irresponsible" programming? Could you please provide specific examples?*

Kate Langrall-Folb: We feel that it's important to give a young person the whole picture when it comes to sexuality. With regard to teen pregnancy, that would mean not just portraying the romance of sex, but also risks and responsibilities that go along with sexual activity, so that young people get a clear picture of what it means to be sexually active. They can better make a decision for their own lives. If all we're doing is telling them that sex is fun and romantic and you get the attention of the boys or whatever, but we don't tell them the other consequences, they're not able to make a responsible decision because they don't have all the information. We're not trying to clean up TV by taking all sexual content off the air, because that's unrealistic. We are asking the industry to paint a more realistic picture for the young people, and that will normalize healthy behaviors and provide them with the information they need to make the best decision for their own lives.

Your organization's literature states that "TV is one of the primary sources for information about sex." Why, since this is the most computer and media savvy generation of young people ever?

Television is still cited as one of the top three to four resources that kids turn to for information about sex. Obviously the computer world has begun to have a role, but if you look at our society as a whole, there are still many young people that do not have computers or are computer literate for that purpose. I expect it will change and computers will become even more influential, but right now [in 2000] young people cite school, parents, and television as their top resources for sex. The fourth is their friends, and there could still be some misinformation conveyed from those two resources.

Providing sex education

Whatever happened to "creative license" and creative freedom? Isn't it the parent's individual responsibility to educate their own children?

Personally, absolutely. I believe that parents should be a very large presence in their young persons' lives, specifically with regard to sexuality. We know this is not the case for a lot of young people. It's not getting discussed in the home. It's not getting taught in school because of the debate in Washington and many schools are adopting the Abstinence Until Marriage message. From our perspective, what's going on in Washington right now is that a lot of money has been appropriated to go to state school boards of education for the purpose of promoting "Abstinence Until Marriage" health education programs. There are several guidelines spelled out that if the state takes the money, they have to teach certain things. They have to say that waiting until you're married is the expected standard, and they can talk about HIV and AIDS or pregnancy as a medical condition, but they cannot teach how to prevent those things from happening. A lot of them do not teach birth control, or they may teach how it works, but they cannot tell you where to go to get them. They cannot tell you any more information about making it available to young people. I'm not the authority on this. The problem arises in that kids are not receiving the whole picture in school either, as far as risks, responsibilities, actions they can take in order to protect themselves. They're being given one message, which is wait until you're married. This does not work for everyone. It's a very one-sided approach and, consequently, kids are not being informed at school. It's not being talked about in the home because parents are not there, they're working, or they are embarrassed, and so kids are looking to TV for the answers. TV is in a unique position because it offers a window. Kids look at it as a window to the adult world, whether it's realistic or not, and they are picking up on cues and behaviors and all of that from TV. If we can work with TV, we try very hard not to infringe on a writer's creative vision for his/her show but rather to say, if you are planning a sexual encounter or even discussion of sex on your show, could you think about portraying the risks and responsibilities as well, or somehow incorporating the other side to this message? We very much respect their creative vision, and I am not a television writer and I'm very much in awe of the creativity in the city of Los Angeles and these people who come up with wonderful stories on a weekly basis. I would not pretend to be able to tell them how to do their job, but to keep them informed and to encourage them to let us see a condom, or let us hear two young people talking about their decision to become sexually active. Things like that that don't change the story but enhance it. . . .

> **"** We feel that it's important to give a young person the whole picture when it comes to sexuality. **"**

There has been a drop in teen pregnancies in the past few years. Has TV played a role in this, either negatively or positively?

I would love to be able to say I have data on that and I would love to say yes, it's played a positive role. My personal opinion is it has, because if you think about it, in the last ten

years, we've started to see condoms being mentioned on TV, or
safer sex slowly becoming more normalized in a young person's
life. A large percentage of the reason why the teen pregnancy
rate has dropped is because young people are using contraceptives more. Just from viewing and from watching TV, you can
see that it has become more normalized on TV, as well as in society and elsewhere. We still have a very long way to go. . . .

Young people are watching and learning

*Now that AIDS education TV specials and safe-sex plot lines are on
the rise, how has that influenced teen sexual behavior?*

I don't have hard data, but my personal feeling is yes. We
did conduct a very unscientific on-line survey of viewers of the
show "Felicity" in which there was an episode where Felicity decides she's ready to become sexually active, and goes to the
health clinic and learns about birth control. Actually on camera,
they demonstrate how to put on a condom on a prop. So we
linked up with three teen-created "Felicity" web sites, and we
asked the kids that came to the site about their viewing habit,
about some other things that had been on the "Felicity" show
that season, and we asked them their opinion of that episode.
Did they think if was informative? How did they feel about seeing a condom demonstration? We had about 100 girls between
ages of 12 and 21 that we tabulated, and 36 out of that 103 girls
said they had never seen a demonstration of the correct way to
use a condom before. Eighty-nine out of that 103 said that teens
get helpful information about sex and birth control from TV.
Sixty said they felt the demonstration of the correct way to use
condom was informative. Twenty-seven said they learned something new about birth control or safer sex from the condom
demonstration episode of "Felicity." It tells us that kids are
watching and are picking up information. We also [surveyed] after a previous episode of "Felicity" which dealt with date rape
(two-part episode). We consulted with the writers extensively
and succeeded in getting them to mention emergency contraception. We also encouraged them to put up an 800 number for
a rape crisis hotline. The hotline received over 1000 calls. This
tells us that young people are watching, learning and, if given
the opportunity to take some action, they will do that.

Where can I find more information about these issues?

I'll give one suggestion to parents. I always tell parents that
first of all, watch what your kids are watching. Sit down with

them and watch it. If you really want to read or get dinner ready, it might be worth your while to sit down and get to know the programs they're watching. Even the bad stuff you can use to spark dialogue with your child. You can say at the commercial, what do you think about the decision that the character made? Even if the character made a decision that the parent disagreed with, the parents can give their perspective, and give their child a chance to consider the differences. It's also helpful because you can relate to that favorite character. What would Felicity have done? Use the stuff that you don't approve of to start a discussion.

10

Television Gives Teens Distorted Information About Sex

James P. Steyer

James P. Steyer, a faculty member at Stanford University in California, is a leading expert in media, education, and child advocacy. His work has been featured on Oprah, *the* Today show, *and in such publications as the* New York Times, Newsweek, *and* Time.

Since the 1970s television producers have increasingly included sexual content in their programs because "sex sells." In 2001, 84 percent of sitcoms contained sexual content. Programs use sex to lure viewers and do not provide a realistic view of the risks involved, including STDs, unwanted pregnancies, and pathological relationships. Parents need to be more responsible in monitoring their children's television viewing.

When it comes to pushing products, the first rule of marketing is that "sex sells." Over the years, that's a lesson that broadcasters, cable companies, music industry executives, and many other media suppliers have learned extremely well. Struggling to compete with one another for profitable "eyeballs," the networks have, decade after decade, pushed the envelope of what they consider acceptable for family viewing. As television journalist Louis Chunovic has ably chronicled, broadcasters have increasingly followed the principle that "there's no better audience grabber than sex."

James P. Steyer, *The Other Parent: The Inside Story of the Media's Effect on Our Children.* New York: Atria Books, 2002. Copyright © 2002 by James P. Steyer. Reproduced by permission of Simon & Schuster Adult Publishing Group.

TV's increasing use of sex

It wasn't always that way. Back in the early 1950s, when the television age dawned, the words "sex" and "pregnancy" were unmentionable on TV, and twin beds were the rule even for the small screen's married couples. Broadcasters voluntarily vowed to keep the airwaves free of "profanity, obscenity, smut, and vulgarity," and their 1951 code of standards ruled that "the use of locations associated with sexual life or with sexual sin must be governed by good taste and delicacy." Even as late as the early 1960s, any TV image of a husband and wife in the same bed had to reveal at least one of the wife's nightgown shoulder straps; not even the subtlest hint of connubial nudity was allowed.

There's no better audience grabber than sex.

But by the mid-1970s, as the sexual revolution exploded, traditional notions of what was permissible in movies, books, theater, and television changed rapidly. TV shows like *All in the Family* began dealing with subjects such as premarital sex, adultery, homosexuality, and pregnancy. Lightly edited feature films were bringing risque content to TV, and explicit sex was suddenly beamed, uninvited, into millions of homes through the new phenomenon of cable television. On public access cable channels after 11:30 P.M., any viewer of any age could stumble onto explicit, hard-core shows like *Midnight Blue*, featuring strippers and prostitutes and hosted by *Screw* magazine publisher Al Goldstein. (I remember flipping the dial one night when I was a teenager and suddenly seeing a set full of porno stars sitting around naked on one of these channels—an eye-opening and unforgettable experience.) After harsh criticisms by Congress and the Federal Communications Commission (FCC), broadcasters voluntarily agreed in 1975 to set aside the 7:00–9:00 P.M. period every evening for shows that were considered appropriate for "family viewing." But even so, despite continued criticism from public-interest and religious groups, prime-time kept pushing the limits, as "jiggle" programs like *Charlie's Angels* and *Three's Company* drew audiences with shows packed with sexual innuendo.

More than anything, however, it was the [Ronald] Reagan administration's deregulation crusade in the 1980s that loosened most of the remaining restraints on broadcast and cable companies, setting the industry off on a downhill race for the bottom line. Ironically, given the fact that the Reagan team was so cozy with [Reverend] Jerry Falwell and the "family values" fundamentalists, one effect of their policy was that new pay cable channels started bringing more X-rated action than ever into American homes. The last barriers came tumbling down in the late 1980s, when a new major television network, Fox Broadcasting, took on the Big Three—CBS, NBC, and ABC—targeting a younger audience with raunchy shows like *Married . . . with Children*. All of a sudden, the lewd, crude Bundys paraded into American homes in the prime-time 7:30 slot, taking family viewing down to a new level.

Anything goes

Since then, it's basically been anything goes. Today, sex is the focus and main plot device of more and more television shows, from the casual bed swapping of *Friends* to the bathroom-stall couplings of *Ally McBeal*. Shows aimed at teen audiences, like *Boston Public*, are every bit as loaded with sexual content. Episodes of that show have featured sex between high school students and faculty members and the confession of one teen that she masturbated while fantasizing about her male teacher. Today, as Syracuse University media professor Robert Thompson points out, "It's commonplace to hear erection jokes on *Friends* at eight o'clock; even gentle little programs like *Everybody Loves Raymond* have the kind of stuff that, when it played on *Three's Company* twenty years ago, made the PTA go completely ballistic." And remember, that's just broadcast television. Cable channels air uncut, R-rated movies, porn, and adult prime-time fare like HBO's *Sex and the City*, available to viewers of all ages in subscribing households.

Kids are watching adult shows

Most of these shows, except for *Boston Public*, aren't targeted at kids, so why should we care about their content? The reason is that children over ten do not limit their TV viewing to *Rugrats*, *Scooby Doo*, and other programs specifically produced for youngsters. Instead, most kids that age spend up to 70 percent of their television time watching adult shows, where sexual content has been skyrocketing.

According to a study by the politically conservative Parents Television Council, sexual material on broadcast television jumped more than 42 percent in just two years, from 1996 to 1998; "plainly put," the report said, "television is the raunchiest it's ever been." Another recent study, released by the Kaiser Family Foundation in 2001, found that over two-thirds of TV shows, including 84 percent of sitcoms, now contain sexual content, up from 56 percent in 1998. For young viewers, it all adds up to an average exposure of more than 14,000 sexual references each year, on TV alone. . . .

Thwarting parents as gatekeepers

Why does it matter? After all, most kids will probably grow up to be normal adults, even after overexposure to sexual media messages. The truth is, it matters for a lot of reasons, and those reasons change as children grow and mature from early childhood into adolescence. At the earliest ages, exposing kids to the media's sexual barrage violates what many parents feel is childhood's precious and protective veil of innocence. Neil Postman, chairman of New York University's Department of Culture and Communication, defines children as "a special class of people . . . requiring special forms of nurturing and protection." It's the parent's role, he argues, to guard them from aspects of life that they are not ready to understand, including sexual relations, violence, illness, and other potentially frightening features of the adult world. Bit by bit, as children grow older and are psychologically able to handle and understand more information, it's the parent's job to expose them to those aspects of life in appropriate and timely ways. Parents are essentially the gatekeepers, introducing children to a sequence of revealed secrets about adult life.

> *Today, sex is the focus and main plot device of more and more television shows.*

I believe most parents understand intuitively what Postman means. We know that young children can be easily scared and confused by behavior that they don't understand, and we struggle to shelter them from those parts of life until they're older. This gatekeeping, in fact, goes to the heart of who we are as parents—and that's exactly what the media is violating. By thrusting increasingly explicit sexual imagery and language at us on television, radio, movie screens, and in advertisements, the media too often exposes our children to those secrets before we think they're ready, shattering our role as gatekeepers and protectors. Too often, parents feel blindsided by the media, surprised and sickened by what their kids have been exposed to, and helpless to control the rate at which their children are pushed into the adult world. . . .

Distorted sexual information

In this overheated cultural climate, kids are not only being exposed to sexual material very early. They are also growing up with unrealistic and distorted information and expectations about sex. Today, the media is very much a teacher—about the world, about judgment, about sexual relations. Children of all ages tend to identify with young, glamorous entertainment stars and use their fictionalized and media-hyped lives as a key source of information about sex. Despite the fact that many parents consider themselves to be their kids' main source of sex education, more and more adolescents say they rely on the media for this knowledge. In fact, according to studies by the Kaiser Family Foundation, thirteen-to-fifteen-year-olds rate the entertainment media as one of the top sources of sexual information, and nearly a quarter of all teens report that they learn "a lot" about birth control and pregnancy from movies and TV. They're absorbing not just "facts," but behaviors and standards, too. Through the media, as psychology researcher L. Monique Ward explains, kids learn social norms and expectations about how to be sexual, who should have sex and when, as well as

> whom to have it with, and what the appropriate sequence of activities is. Through its themes, storylines, characterizations, and dialogue, [the media] provides insight into these sexual scripts, depicting various aspects about attracting and selecting partners, dating and sexual decision making. Watching is an eager audience of children and adolescents who may have little experience of their own and minimal input from other sources to which they can compare these portrayals.

As Ward points out, the media's most frequent message about sex is that it's a form of recreation—a competitive, manipulative "sport" emphasizing physical appearance and "momentary, high-sensation pleasures." Many teens don't get a counterbalancing message, since parents are often reluctant to talk about sexual issues, and most schools and religious organizations don't provide these guidelines. From the stories that the media tells kids—packaged and distorted for maximum marketing effect—children learn patterns of behavior in what some researchers refer to as "stalagmite effects—cognitive deposits built up almost imperceptibly from the drip-drip-drip" of repeated exposure over time.

During early adolescence especially—an age when children go through rapid physical and emotional changes, have less contact with adults, and make the challenging transition out of elementary school—they are turning to the media for role models for behavior, decision making, and sex. Adolescence is a time, explained Dr. Jacqueline Eccles, a psychology professor at the University of Michigan, "when our children need to figure out who they are and what is their place in the larger society"—and today that perception is shaped, in significant measure, by media messages.

Television is the raunchiest it's ever been.

Those messages are confusing. Even teen magazines that steer their editorial focus away from sex lace their pages with provocative ads—like Calvin Klein's images of teens in underwear and Levi's ads showing a boy's face pressed against the crotch of a woman's jeans. Brandon Holley, editor of *ELLEgirl*, acknowledged that "this demographic is bombarded by sex images," and the influence of those images starts early. As one nineteen-year-old girl reflected, "I don't recall having sexuality pushed in my face when I was ten or eleven. But I have a younger half-sister who is eleven years old, and she's a very big fan of Britney Spears and the Spice Girls, and she tries to emulate them. . . . I see her wanting to wear clothes that I would never have considered wearing."

Boys don't escape these powerful influences. While girls have long suffered from anxiety about their bodies, boys are catching up, thanks to increasingly glamorized and sexualized images of young males in advertising and the entertainment media. One recent Calvin Klein newspaper and billboard ad, for instance, featured an image of a muscled boy of about seventeen, wearing nothing but revealingly clingy white bikini underwear. Thanks in part to widely hyped media images like these, some boys are now struggling with what some call an "Adonis complex," trying to burn baby fat and build six-pack abs in order to look cool and sexually attractive. When advertisers use sexualized teenage bodies to sell products, they create images and expectations that are frustratingly impossible for most teenagers to live up to.

> *Despite the fact that many parents consider themselves to be their kids' main source of sex education, more and more adolescents say they rely on the media for this knowledge.*

The media's relentless emphasis on sex also shapes expectations and behaviors. In one study, teens said their top two sources of sexual pressure were television shows and music. As fourteen-year-old Rayelyn Rodriguez explained it, some TV shows "tell kids 'Everybody's doing it.' Then some kids think, 'Well, if everyone's doing it, why don't I?'" Drew Pinsky, MD, an expert who talks to a lot of teens on his popular call-in show *Loveline*, aired on radio and MTV, is convinced that extensive early exposure to sexually charged material can have a negative effect on kids. "Premature exposure to sexual material tends to be sexualizing," he has said, for children who are not psychologically mature enough to handle it. The opposite is also true. Kids who get most of their information about sex from their parents, not the media, tend to be less sexually active overall. Eight-to-twelve-year-old kids, in fact, would rather hear about sex and relationships from their parents and trust their parents more than other sources.

Risky business

A steady diet of media sex can have other troubling effects on adolescents. The fact is that while sex is pervasive in the media, it is rarely accompanied by any discussion of the risks and consequences of sexual behavior. These risks are real for American teenagers today. The rate of teen pregnancy in the United States, while it has declined in recent years, is still double that in Europe and nine times that in Japan, and sexually transmitted diseases (STDs) are on the rise. One quarter of sexually active teens—about four million kids—are infected with STDs each year, and the highest rates of gonorrhea and chlamydia are among teens between the ages of fifteen and nineteen. The most alarming news is that AIDS ranks sixth as the leading cause of death for young people between fifteen and twenty-four. Twenty percent of those who have AIDS are in their twenties, and the majority were infected as teenagers.

These are critical health issues for teens and anyone who is sexually active, but they are rarely addressed by the number-one source of sex information, the media. As seventeen-year-old Gaines Newborn of Los Angeles observed, "Shows like *Dawson's Creek* bring out a lot of sex questions that kids want to know [about], but they don't answer them." When television and movies do manage to address sexual issues in age-appropriate ways, with realistic information about choices, responsibilities, and consequences, they can help teens sort through the facts and make positive choices. Too often, though, the entertainment media use sexual content as attention-getting bait to lure viewers, with no discussion whatever of risks and responsibilities. "Surveys tell us young people get a lot of their information about sex from TV," notes Drew Altman, president and chief executive of the Henry J. Kaiser Family Foundation, a health and media research organization. "With the problems facing adolescents today, how sex is shown on TV is just as important as how much sex is shown."

Extensive early exposure to sexually charged material can have a negative effect on kids.

The reason, points out Lynn Ponton, MD—a psychoanalyst and professor at the University of California, San Francisco—is that sex is an area of life that is fraught with risk, and "most adolescents," she notes, "don't yet have well-developed risk-assessment skills." Encouraged by the media environment, teens are not only having sex earlier—at the average age of six-teen—"but they are taking greater risks in this area," she adds. Continually exposed to images of unprotected sex, teens may downplay the risk of such behavior—"with consequences that include sexually transmitted disease, unwanted pregnancy, and pathological relationships, among others."

Teens want to fit in

In a candid article in one high school newspaper, for example, teens recently talked frankly about the pressure they feel to have casual sex. Due in large measure to the media's influence, a tenth-grade girl reported, kids are "obsessed with sex" and "aren't prepared for what they are actually getting themselves into," she said. "The emotional connection doesn't have to be there," an eleventh-grade boy added; "no one has any expecta-tion beyond a one-night stand," reported a ninth-grade girl. Sex—especially oral sex—"is meaningless, just for fun"—like "going out and having a soda," another student stated. For some, however, there is an emotional price. One boy described parties where tenth-graders drank a lot and had casual sex in or-der to fit in; afterward, he'd see girls "just sitting there crying and touching their stomachs," realizing what they had just done. In a media climate that promotes recreational sex to grab audiences, teens are growing up with risky attitudes and habits that could harm them—physically, psychologically, and emo-tionally—down the road. "I believe we have let our teenagers down in this area," Ponton states. "We may provide condoms, but we don't offer conversations." Instead, we set kids loose in a media culture that defines sex as a game. "It's all about getting what you want quicker and easier," one teenager remarked.

Parental responsibility

By undermining parents' gatekeeping role, providing unrealis-tic information about sex, and persuading kids that sexual risk-taking is less serious than it really is, the media is not only de-stroying kids' innocence too soon but is also setting them up for disappointment and dangerous choices. What's missing in this mix is adult responsibility and restraint. Parents aren't con-trolling, or effectively influencing, their kids' media environ-ment. And the companies that create and distribute media for our consumption are interested primarily, sometimes exclusively, in the profitability of their commercial products. The values of the media, as John Condry argued, "are the values of the marketplace." It cannot, he said, "be a useful source of information for children. Indeed, it may be a dangerous source of information. It offers ideas that are false, unreal; it has no coherent value system, other than consumerism; it provides little useful information about the self."

11

Parents Should Be Consulted Before Teens Are Given Contraceptive Services

U.S. Conference of Catholic Bishops

The U.S. Conference of Catholic Bishops (USCCB) is an organization based in Washington, D.C., that promotes Catholicism and provides charitable and educational services.

Title X is a federally funded program that provides low-income women with contraceptive services. Over a million teenagers receive free prescription contraceptives from the program and may do so without their parents' knowledge or consent. This lack of parental notification is wrong. Parents have the right and responsibility to care for their children, and the government should not usurp that role. Furthermore, the government should not send the message that premarital sex is acceptable, which is what many clinics in the Title X program do.

What is the Title X program?

Title X of the Public Health Service Act was established as a federal program in 1970. For many years it has offered low income women certain "reproductive health" services, including family planning as well as "non-directive" pregnancy counseling and referrals on all "options," including abortion. By law, abortion may not be treated as a method of family planning in the program; yet abortion referrals are *mandated* by Public Health Service guidelines governing the program.

> **❝**Most forms of contraceptives have potentially dangerous side effects for young women.**❞**

This year [2003], the Title X program is slated to receive $203 million from the federal government to fund approximately 4,800 state or county health departments, independent clinics, and Planned Parenthood affiliates across the country (known as "grantees"). In 1996, Planned Parenthood affiliates received $46.4 million in Title X funds, according to the Government Accounting Office (GAO). Planned Parenthood is strongly opposed to parental consent or notification laws, which, in its view, interfere with the "confidential" relationship between its counselors and unemancipated minors.

One-third of the approximately five million women served by the program are teenagers. Unmarried teens may qualify for free services regardless of their parents' income or consent. Currently, a teenager may walk into any Title X clinic and receive free prescription contraceptives, including potentially harmful implants or injectables like Norplant and Depo-Provera, without her parents' knowledge or consent.

Contraceptives can be harmful and ineffective

Most forms of contraceptives have potentially dangerous side effects for young women, which parents—not clinic workers—are left to deal with. None of these drugs and devices shields against sexually transmitted diseases. Some, such as Norplant, Depo-Provera and the low-estrogen Pill may sometimes act as abortifacients [agents that induce abortions] by preventing the embryo from implanting in the womb. Others, such as "emergency contraception" (sometimes called the "morning-after" pill, though actually taken up to 72 hours after intercourse), have this abortifacient effect as their *primary* mode of action.

Teen contraceptive use does not reduce abortions. A 1986 study found that despite large national expenditures for family planning for 15–19 year olds, both pregnancy rates and abortion rates rose over time. The researchers compared 1971 (federal, state and local) expenditures at $11 million with 1981 figures of $400 million (including Title X funds). With the teen population about the same in each year, in 1972 the pregnancy rate for 15–19 year olds was 95 per 1,000 and in 1981 the rate was 113. During that same time, the abortion rate rose from 190,000 to 430,000. (Stan Weed, "Curbing Births, Not Pregnancies," *The Wall Street Journal*, Oct. 14, 1986.) Further, according to the Alan Guttmacher Institute, most women having abortions were using contraceptives when they became pregnant. Contraceptive effectiveness is even lower among teens.

Why parental notification is needed

Recent national statistics show that teen sexual activity, pregnancy rates, and abortion rates are declining for a variety of reasons. The messages we send to our teens should encourage this trend by stressing the dangers of premature sexual activity. Parents are the most appropriate and reliable people to send such a message. Many Title X grantees send the opposite message.

In a 1996 Henry J. Kaiser Family Foundation survey of 1,500 teens (ages 12–18), 55% said their parents are the source they trust for the most "reliable and complete" information about sex and birth control. The next highest category was the 39% who said they trust a doctor or nurse; 9 percent trust a family planning clinic.

> *Teen contraceptive use does not reduce abortions.*

In a widely cited example in 1997, a 37-year-old Crystal Lake, IL teacher was convicted of criminal sexual assault and child pornography for having an 18-month affair with his 14-year-old student. He had been taking her to the local health department, funded by Title X, where she received injections of Depo-Provera, so he could continue to abuse her without her parent's knowledge. The teacher is serving a sentence of ten years, and the health department voted not to accept Title X funds next year [2004].

This shocking example, and the overall lack of parental notification in the Title X program, are affronts to parents' rightful role as the primary educators of their children. Government agencies or counselors cannot replace and should not interfere with the rights and responsibilities of loving parents, particularly in sensitive matters dealing with human sexuality and the transmission of human life. Government should protect the role of loving and supportive parents, and make it possible to terminate the parental rights of those who abuse their trust. Current policy does just the opposite: Pushing parents out of the situation, and protecting abusers.

12

Requiring Parental Consent for Contraceptive Services Puts Teens at Risk

National Family Planning and Reproductive Health Association

The National Family Planning and Reproductive Health Association is a nonprofit organization established to assure access to reproductive health care services, including contraceptives, abortion, and STD testing.

Title X of the Public Health Service Act is a federally funded program that provides confidential and low-cost family planning services, including a variety of contraceptives, counseling, and testing for sexually transmitted diseases (STDs). Legislators continue to propose amendments to Title X that would require parental consent or notification before adolescents could receive these services. Studies have shown that more than 50 percent of teenagers would forgo family planning services and medical treatment if their parents had to be notified, thus jeopardizing teens' health and raising the rates of unintended pregnancies and STDs, including HIV/AIDS.

Confidential access to family planning is crucial in helping teenagers obtain timely medical advice and appropriate medical care. Title X of the Public Health Service Act is the nation's family planning program and has been a critical component in efforts to reduce teen pregnancy and STD rates. Each year, publicly funded family planning services help teenagers to avoid almost 400,000 unintended pregnancies and provide STD counseling and testing to thousands of teens. Teen pregnancies would have been 20% higher during the past two decades without publicly funded family planning services. . . .

Health risks

Studies indicate that requiring parental consent or notification for young people to receive family planning or other health care services will mean that many teens delay or avoid seeking those services, placing them at risk for unwanted, unplanned pregnancies as well as sexually transmitted diseases (STDs) including HIV/AIDS. When minors delay diagnosis and treatment for STDs or HIV, the minors' health, future fertility, and even life can be put at risk.

Parental consent requirements will result in increased rates of unintended pregnancies, abortion, as well as STDs and HIV. Statistics bear out the need for more, not less access to contraceptive and STD screening and treatment services. However, there remains a great deal of room for improvement. Despite declining teen pregnancy rates, four in ten girls become pregnant at least once before age 20. Seventy-eight percent of teen pregnancies in the United States are unintended and a staggering three million teens—approximately one in four sexually active youth—acquire an STD each year. For the vast majority of these teens, parental consent requirements would not have the effect of reducing teens' sexual activity but instead would deter them from behaving responsibly and seeking much needed, sensitive health services. . . .

How teens would respond

• A study published in the August 14, 2002 issue of the *Journal of the American Medical Association (JAMA)* found that 59% of the teens in their survey—nearly 6 in 10—said that knowing their parents would be notified would prevent them from seeking family planning services. Amazingly, 99% said they would still have sex.

• In the year following the elimination of a parental consent requirement for HIV testing in Connecticut, the number of teens aged 13–17 obtaining HIV tests doubled.

• Fifty-eight percent of high school students surveyed in three public schools in Massachusetts reported having health concerns that they did not want to share with their parents. Approximately 25% of the students said they would forego medical treatment if disclosure of treatment to their parents were a possibility.

> *Parental consent requirements would not have the effect of reducing teens' sexual activity but instead would deter them from behaving responsibly.*

• Another study of adolescents found that if confidential treatment for sexually transmitted diseases were available, 50% of the adolescents would seek care. Only 15% reported that they would do so if parental consent or notice were required.

Those in opposition

Leading medical and public health groups, including the American College of Obstetricians and Gynecologists, the American Academy of Pediatrics, the American Academy of Family Physicians, the American Public Health Association, the American Medical Women's Association, and the National Medical Association oppose mandatory parental notification or consent requirements in order for young people to obtain family planning services. Also, an American Medical Association (AMA) policy statement from 1993 indicates that the AMA "oppose(s) regulations that require parental notification when prescription contraceptives are provided to minors through federally funded programs, since they create a breach of confidentiality in the physician-patient relationship. Obstacles to the distribution of birth control information, medication, and devices should be removed, and physicians should provide contraceptive services on a confidential basis where legally permissible."

Teens using services are already sexually active

The vast majority of teens seeking services at a Title X clinic are already sexually active. Levels of teen sexual activity show no correlation to the availability of confidential reproductive health care. Confidential access to health care services does not "cause" non-sexually active adolescents to start having sex. On average, teens are sexually active for 14 months prior to making a family planning visit. One study of over 1,200 teenagers in 31 family planning clinics showed that only 14% of teens came in for family planning services prior to initiating sexual activity. Over one-third of teens (36%) sought services only because they suspected they were pregnant. . . .

Confidentiality is important to teens

Allowing parental consent or notification for even one service offered at a Title X clinic will have the effect of deterring teens from seeking any services. Title X family planning clinics offer a wide range of services including contraception, screening and treatment for STDs, HIV screening, routine gynecological exams, and breast and cervical cancer screening. If teens are required to have written parental consent or know their parents will be notified prior to their receiving contraceptive services, not only will they avoid seeking family planning services, they will avoid seeking any services at a Title X clinic.

Title X strikes the right balance by encouraging parental involvement but not requiring parental consent or notification. Under Title X guidelines, adolescents must be assured that the counseling sessions are confidential and, if follow-up is necessary, every attempt must be made to assure the privacy of the individual. However, counselors are required to encourage family participation in the decision of minors to seek family planning services and provide counseling to minors on resisting attempts to coerce minors into engaging in sexual activities.

Access to contraceptive services is vital

Erecting roadblocks for teens attempting to behave responsibly is counter to the national goal of reducing unintended pregnancy and limiting disease. Recent declines in the teen pregnancy and teen abortion rates have been attributed to increased use of birth control along with some decrease in the rate of teen sexual activity. A 1999 analysis by The Alan Guttmacher Institute reports that approximately 75% of the decline in the teen pregnancy rate between 1988 and 1995 reflect improved contraceptive use among sexually active teenagers; 25% is due to reduced sexual activity. In addition, teenagers in the United States continue to experience substantially higher pregnancy rates and birthrates than teens in other Western industrialized countries because of lower contraceptive use. The adolescent pregnancy rate in the United States is nearly twice that in Canada and Great Britain and approximately four times that in France and Sweden. Moreover, teen birthrates have declined less steeply in the United States than in other developed countries over the last three decades. Sexually active teens in the United States are less likely to use any contraceptive method and especially less likely to use highly effective hormonal methods, primarily the pill, than their peers in other countries.

> *Confidential access to health care services does not 'cause' non-sexually active adolescents to start having sex.*

Allowing states to impose mandatory parental involvement does not achieve the intended benefit of promoting family communication. Many teens initially involve a parent or other adult in their decision to seek family planning services while others, after counseling, will bring a parent or other adult with them on subsequent clinic visits. However, requiring parental consent before a teen receives prescription drugs could cause some young people, who may be alienated from their parents or fear abuse, to delay or avoid making responsible decisions, like using contraception.

The link between poverty and teen childbearing is profound and long lasting:

• Half of all single mothers on welfare were teenagers when they had their first child.

• Less than one-third of teen mothers ever finish high school, leaving many unprepared for the job market and more likely to raise their children in poverty.

• Children of teen mothers are twice as likely to be abused and neglected as are children of older mothers.

• The children of teen mothers tend to bear the greatest burden of teen pregnancy. They are more likely to do poorly in school, more likely to drop out of school, and less likely to attend college. The consequences to the children of teen mothers continue into young adulthood.

• Girls born to teen mothers are 22 percent more likely to become mothers as teens themselves.

Parental consent/notification would disproportionately impact low-income teens who cannot afford needed services at a private physician's office. Young women who can afford services will continue to have access to confidential care—the burden will fall on young low-income women who depend on affordable prescription contraceptives to avoid pregnancy.

13

Abstinence Is the Best Message for Teens

Bridget E. Maher

Bridget E. Maher is a policy analyst with the Family Research Council, an organization that provides the nation's lawmakers with critical research on public policy affecting marriage and family. She researches, writes, and offers expert commentary on the issues of marriage, divorce, cohabitation, and adoption.

The majority of public schools teach "comprehensive" sex education, believing that kids will inevitably have sex and therefore need information about it. Abstinence-until-marriage programs, on the other hand, teach teens that premarital sexual activity is not acceptable, and that abstinence is the only foolproof method of preventing unwanted pregnancies and STDs. These classes include lessons designed to help students improve their decision-making skills, boost their self-esteem, and resist the pressure to have sex. Abstinence education programs have been successful in many states.

Public opinion polls show that teens value abstinence highly. Nearly all (93 percent) of teenagers believe that teens should be given a strong message from society to abstain from sex until at least after high school. A 2000 poll found that 64 percent of teen girls surveyed said sexual activity is not acceptable for high-school age adolescents, even if precautions are taken to prevent pregnancy and sexually transmitted diseases. Moreover, teens who have not abstained often regret being sexually active. In 2000, 63 percent of sexually active teens said they wish they had waited longer to become sexually active.

The negative consequences of unwed teen sex

Teens need to be taught to save sex for marriage, because premarital sex has many negative consequences, both physical and emotional. One of the most obvious outcomes of engaging in premarital sex is having a child outside marriage; today, one-third of all births are out-of-wedlock. Teen birthrates have declined since the early 1990s, but the highest unwed birthrates are among those age 20–24, followed by those 25–29. This shows that many young girls abstain from sex while they are in high school, but not afterward.

> *// Teens need to be taught to save sex for marriage, because premarital sex has many negative consequences, both physical and emotional. //*

Teen unwed childbearing has negative consequences for mothers, children, and society. Unwed teen mothers are likely to live in poverty and be dependent on welfare, and only about 50 percent of them are likely to finish high school while they are adolescents or young adults. Children born to teen mothers are more likely than other children to have lower grades, to leave high school without graduating, to be abused or neglected, to have a child as an unmarried teenager, and to be delinquent. Teen childbearing costs U.S. taxpayers an estimated $7 billion per year in social services and lost tax revenue due to government dependency. The gross annual cost to society of unwed childbearing and its consequences is $29 billion, which includes the administration of welfare and foster care programs, building and maintaining additional prisons, as well as lower education and resultant lost productivity among unwed parents.

Aside from the risk of pregnancy, teens have a high risk of contracting a sexually transmitted disease (STD). Each year 3 million teens—25 percent of sexually active teens—are infected with an STD. About 25 percent of all new cases of STDs occur in teenagers; two-thirds of new cases occur in young people age 15–24.

Chlamydia and gonorrhea are two of the most common curable STDs among sexually active teens. According to the

Centers for Disease Control [CDC], gonorrhea rates are highest among 15- to 19-year-old females and 20- to 24-year-old males, and more than 5 to 10 percent of teen females are currently infected with chlamydia. If these diseases are untreated, they can lead to pelvic inflammatory disease, infertility, and ectopic pregnancy. Studies have found that up to 15 percent of sexually active teenage women are infected with the human papillomavirus (HPV), an incurable virus that is present in nearly all cervical cancers.

In addition to being at risk for STDs, unwed sexually active teens are likely to experience negative emotional consequences and to become both more promiscuous and less interested in marriage. Teens who engage in premarital sex are likely to experience fear about pregnancy and STDs, regret, guilt, lowered self-respect, fear of commitment, and depression. Also, adolescents who engage in unwed sex at a younger age are much more likely to have multiple sex partners. Among young people between the ages of 15–24 who have had sex before age 18, 75 percent had two or more partners and 45 percent had four or more partners. Among those who first had sex after age 19, just 20 percent had more than one partner and one percent had four or more partners. Premarital sex can also cause teens to view marriage less favorably. A 1994 study of college freshmen found that non-virgins with multiple sex partners were more likely to view marriage as difficult and involving a loss of personal freedom and happiness. Virgins were more likely to view marriage as "enjoyable.". . .

"Safe sex" programs encourage sexual activity

Teens are also affected by the messages on sex and abstinence that they receive in school. Unfortunately, the majority of schools teach "safe sex," "comprehensive," or so-called "abstinence plus" programs, believing that it is best for children to have all the information they need about sexuality and to make their own decisions about sex. Abstinence is downplayed and sexual activity and condom use are encouraged in these curriculums, because it is assumed that kids are eventually going to have sex. A 2002 report by the Physicians Consortium, which investigated comprehensive sex programs promoted by the Centers for Disease Control, reveals that abstinence is barely mentioned and condom use is clearly advocated in these curriculums. Not only do students learn how to obtain condoms, but they also practice putting them on cucumbers or penile models. Masturbation, body massages, bathing together, and fantasizing are listed as "ways to be close" in one curriculum.

> //*Abstinence is downplayed and sexual activity and condom use are encouraged in these curriculums, because it is assumed that kids are eventually going to have sex. //*

Under a grant from the CDC, the Sexuality Information and Education Council of the United States (SIECUS) developed guidelines for comprehensive sex education, which according to SIECUS, are "the most widely recognized and implemented framework for comprehensive sexuality education across the country." These guidelines call for teaching five-through eight-year-olds about masturbation and accepting cohabitation and homosexuality. Upper elementary and junior high grades have classes on these subjects, as well as lessons on sexual fantasies, contraception, and abortion. For high school students, SIECUS recommends adding discussion on using erotic photographs and literature, body massages, bathing/ showering together, and oral, vaginal, and anal intercourse. Nearly all of the fifty-page guidelines are devoted to these topics, while only one-half of a page is dedicated to abstinence.

The effectiveness of abstinence-until-marriage programs

Abstinence-until-marriage programs, on the other hand, teach young people to save sex for marriage, and their message has been very effective in changing teens' behavior. According to the Physicians Resource Council, the drop in teen birth rates during the 1990s was due not to increased contraceptive use among teens, but to sexual abstinence. This correlates with the decrease in sexual activity among unwed teens. In 1988, 51 percent of unwed girls between the ages of 15 and 19 had engaged in sexual intercourse compared to 49 percent in 1995. This decrease also occurred among unwed boys, declining from 60 percent to 55 percent between 1988 and 1995.

There are over one thousand abstinence-until-marriage

programs around the United States, and one-third of public middle and high schools say both that abstinence is "the main message in their sex education" and that abstinence is taught as "the only option for young people." Started by non-profit or faith-based groups, these programs teach young people to save sex for marriage. However, abstinence organizations do more than just tell teens to say no to unwed sex: They teach young people the skills they need to practice abstinence. Classes cover many topics including self-esteem building, self-control, decision making, goal setting, character education, and communication skills. Sexually transmitted diseases, the realities of parenthood and anatomy are also discussed. The effectiveness of birth control may be discussed, but it is neither provided nor promoted in these programs.

> *Classes cover many topics including self-esteem building, self-control, decision making, goal setting, character education, and communication skills.*

Choosing the Best, an abstinence program based in Marietta, Georgia, and started in 1993, has developed curriculum and materials that are used in over two thousand school districts in 48 states. Students in public or private schools are taught abstinence by their teachers, who have been trained by Choosing the Best's staff. Appropriate for 6th through 12th graders, the curriculum teaches students the consequences of premarital sex, the benefits of abstaining until marriage, how to make a virginity pledge, refusal skills, and character education. Choosing the Best involves parents in their children's lessons and teaches them how to teach abstinence to their children.

Longitudinal studies conducted by Northwestern University Medical School in 1996 and 1999 found many positive results among students who participated in classes using Choosing the Best's curriculum. In 1996, 54 percent of the teens who were recently sexually active before participating in the program were no longer sexually active one year later. The 1999 study revealed positive changes in teens' attitudes toward sex. On the pretest administered before the abstinence classes, 58 percent of the teens agreed with the statement, "A teen who has had sex outside of marriage would be better off to stop having sex and wait until they are married," while 71 percent agreed on the post-test. Also, agreement with the statement "The best way for me to keep from getting AIDS or some sexually transmitted disease is to wait until I am married before having sex" went from 71 percent before the course to 84 percent afterwards.

This abstinence program has also contributed to lower teen-pregnancy rates in Georgia. In Columbus, Georgia, Choosing the Best's materials were used in all 8th grades for a period of four years. A study requested by the Georgia State Board of Education to examine the effectiveness of this curriculum found a 38-percent reduction in pregnancies among middle-school students in Muscogee County between 1997 and 1999. Other large school districts that did not implement Choosing the Best's program experienced only a 6-percent reduction in teen pregnancies during those same years.

Teen-Aid, Inc., based in Spokane, Washington, has been promoting abstinence until marriage and character education for over twenty years. This program seeks to teach young people the knowledge and skills they need to make good decisions and to achieve goals. Parent-child communication is a key component of the Teen-Aid curriculum, as parents are involved in every lesson. In 1999–2000, over 41,000 families in public schools, churches, and community organizations used these materials.

> *Teens who take a virginity pledge are 34 percent less likely to have sex before marriage compared to those who do not pledge.*

A 1999 study conducted by Whitworth College in Spokane, Washington found many positive results among teens in Edinburg, Texas who were taught the Teen-Aid curriculum. On the pretest administered to students before the course, 62 percent said "having sex as a teenager would make it harder for them to get a good job or be successful in a career," compared to 71 percent on the post-test. When asked if they were less likely to have sexual intercourse before they got married, 47 percent responded yes on the pretest, compared to 54 percent after taking the course. The Teen-Aid curriculum was also successful at teaching students when human life begins. Before taking the course, 38 percent believed that "a baby is a person or a human being at conception," compared to 47 percent who agreed with this statement after participating in the program.

Character building

The Art of Loving Well Project, a character education program, has also been very effective in teaching abstinence. Developed at Boston University, *The Art of Loving Well* is a 340-page anthology of literature selections that is used to teach students how to have good relationships. This curriculum was field tested for over four years and is being used successfully throughout the country.

The Office of Adolescent Pregnancy Programs, which has partly funded this project, commissioned an evaluation of it that found many positive results. For example, students who used *The Art of Loving Well* were more likely than the control group to agree with the statements "I intend to say 'no' if I am being pressured to have sex" and "Teens who don't pressure their partner to have sex are showing respect for themselves and their partners." Also, among those who reported being virgins on the pretest, only 8 percent reported having sex on the post-test compared to 28 percent in the control group.

Operation Keepsake, a Cleveland, Ohio–based abstinence program started in 1988, has its "For Keeps" curriculum in 90 public and private schools in the greater Cleveland area. It is presently taught to over 25,000 students, including those in middle and high school, as well as college freshmen. Along with a classroom component, this program also includes peer mentoring, guest speakers, opportunities to make an abstinence pledge, and parental involvement.

Case Western Reserve University evaluated Operation Keepsake's program in 2001, finding that it is having a positive impact on adolescents' beliefs and behavior regarding abstinence. Over nine hundred 7th and 8th graders completed the pretests and post-tests. According to the study, the program had "a clear and sustainable impact on abstinence beliefs" because students in the program had "higher abstinence-until-marriage values" at the follow-up survey than did those in the control group, who did not attend the abstinence program. Among those students who were sexually experienced, 55 percent of those who participated in Operation Keepsake's program were abstinent at the follow-up survey compared to 43 percent in the control group.

Virginity pledges encourage sexual abstinence

Virginity pledges are also successful in encouraging sexual abstinence among unwed teens. A 2001 study based on the National Longitudinal Study of Adolescent Health demonstrated the effectiveness of the virginity pledge. The study found that teens who take a virginity pledge are 34 percent less likely to have sex before marriage compared to those who do not pledge, even after controlling for factors such as family structure, race, self-esteem, and religiosity. Also, the 1997 Adolescent Health Study, a longitudinal survey of over 12,000 adolescents in grades seven through twelve, found that adolescents who made a virginity pledge "were at significantly lower risk of early age of sexual debut."

These are only some of the many abstinence-until-marriage programs in the United States. Their success in changing young people's views and behavior regarding abstinence is due to their telling the truth about sex to young people: that it is meant to be saved for marriage and that it is possible to live a chaste life. Along with this message, they give kids the encouragement and skills they need to save themselves for marriage.

14

Abstinence-Only Sex Education Endangers Students

National Coalition Against Censorship

The National Coalition Against Censorship (NCAC), founded in 1974, is an alliance of fifty national nonprofit organizations, including literary, artistic, religious, educational, professional, labor, and civil liberties groups. NCAC campaigns for access to information and the free interchange of ideas.

Sex education programs that teach only abstinence fail to educate students about responsible sexual behavior and deny students their right of access to important medical information about sex. The abstinence-only approach has led school boards to censor material in textbooks. Furthermore, teachers have been disciplined or threatened with lawsuits for speaking candidly about sexual matters. As a result, teens are engaging in sexual activities without a basic knowledge of contraception, sexually transmitted diseases, safe sex practices, and abortion.

Abstinence-only education is one of the religious right's greatest victories. But it is only one tactic in a broader, longer-term strategy. Since the early 1980s, the "family values" movement has won the collaboration of governments and public institutions, from Congress to local school boards, in abridging students' constitutional rights. Schools now block student access to sexual information in class, at the school library, and through the public library's Internet portals. They violate students' free speech rights by censoring student publications of ar-

National Coalition Against Censorship, "Abstinence-Only Education: Why First Amendment Supporters Should Oppose It," www.ncac.org, June 2, 2001. Copyright © 2001 by the National Coalition Against Censorship. Reproduced by permission.

ticles referring to sexuality. In abstinence-only classes, instructors force-feed students religious ideology that condemns homosexuality, masturbation, abortion, and sometimes even contraception.

Religion invades public schools

In 1981, Congress passed the Adolescent Family Life Act [AFLA], also known as the "chastity law," which funded educational programs to "promote self-discipline and other prudent approaches" to adolescent sex, or "chastity education." Grant applications to create such programs poured in, and the dollars poured out—to churches and religious conservatives nationwide. The ACLU [American Civil Liberties Union] challenged AFLA in court, calling it a Trojan horse smuggling the values of the Christian Right—particularly its opposition to abortion—to public-school children at public expense: a classic affront to the principle of separation of church and state.

> *Schools now block student access to sexual information in class, at the school library, and through the public library's Internet portals.*

A dozen years later, the Supreme Court held that funded programs must delete direct references to religion (for instance, the suggestion that students take Christ on a date as chaperone), and the granting process was reined in. But it was too late. Some of the biggest federal grant recipients, including Sex Respect and Teen-Aid, had already turned their curricula into robust for-profit businesses. Christian fundamentalist groups, which built much of that infrastructure, remain among the most vehement opponents of comprehensive sexuality education today.

In 1996, Congress struck again, attaching a provision to welfare legislation that established a federal program to fund programs teaching abstinence-until-marriage exclusively. Approximately $100 million, including matching state funds, is spent annually on state programs that have as their "exclusive purpose, teaching the social, psychological, and health gains to be realized by abstaining from sexual activity."

Abstinence-only education
censors crucial instruction

Congress . . . re-authorized funding for abstinence-only education, and a similar trend is also apparent at the state level, where legislatures are copying the federal abstinence-only statute, often adding explicit prior-restraint provisions. A recent proposal in New Jersey, for instance, would impose close surveillance on teaching materials—and teachers. Even if they don't pass, these bills have a censorial and chilling effect. Utah's governor vetoed a similar bill in that state, but directed state agencies to monitor sex-ed programs for "inappropriate" language and subject matter.

Here are a few examples of the problems created by the abstinence-only approach to sex "education":

• Public funds go to religious institutions for *anti*-sex education. In Montana, the Catholic diocese of Helena received $14,000 from the state's Department of Health & Human Services for classes in the "Assets for Abstinence." In Louisiana, a network of pastors is bringing the abstinence-only message to religious congregations with public funds, and the Governor's Program on Abstinence is appointing regional coordinators and other staff members from such religious organizations as the Baptist Collegiate Ministries, Rapides Station Community Ministries, Diocese of Lafayette, Revolution Ministries, Caring to Love Ministries, All Saints Crusade Foundation, Concerned Christian Women of Livingston, Catholic Charities, Christian Counseling Center, and Community Christian Concern.

> *The school board in Franklin County, North Carolina, ordered three chapters literally sliced out of a ninth-grade health textbook.*

• Public schools host "chastity" events. In California, Pennsylvania, Alabama, and many other states, schools regularly host chastity pledges and rallies on school premises during school hours. During these rituals, students often pledge "to God" that they will remain abstinent until they marry.

• Textbooks are censored. The school board in Franklin County, North Carolina, ordered three chapters literally sliced out of a ninth-grade health textbook because the material did not adhere to state law mandating abstinence-only education. The chapters covered AIDS and other STDs [sexually transmitted diseases], marriage and partnering, and contraception. In Lynchburg, Virginia, school board members refused to approve a high-school science textbook unless an illustration of a vagina was covered or cut out.

• Crucial health programs are canceled. In response to a petition from 28 parents, a highly regarded comprehensive AIDS-prevention presentation for high-school students in the Syracuse, New York, area, given by the local AIDS Task Force, was canceled for future students. In Illinois, critics blasted a Centers for Disease Control program, called "Reducing the Risk," because they claim it is inconsistent with an abstinence-only message.

> *The vast majority of American parents support comprehensive sex education.*

• Sex-ed teachers are disciplined for doing their jobs. In Belton, Missouri, a seventh-grade health teacher was suspended when a parent complained that she had discussed "inappropriate" sexual matters in class. The teacher had answered a student's query about oral sex. In Orlando, Florida, a teacher was suspended when he showed a student-made videotape called *Condom Man and his K-Y Commandos*, about preventing AIDS transmission.

• Teachers are threatened with lawsuits; student journalists intimidated. In Granite Bay, California, an article in the student paper prompted charges that a sex-ed teacher engaged in "sexual misconduct" and threats of a lawsuit against the teacher and the paper's faculty adviser. The article took the position that newly mandated abstinence-only education was doing nothing to stop either sexual activity or widespread sexual ignorance among students. In Santa Clarita, California, a high-school principal censored the student paper from printing an article entitled "Sex: Raw and Uncensored." The article was actually about the benefits of abstinence and methods of safe sex.

• Students suffer from ignorance. Comprehensive sex education is becoming the exception rather than the rule; as a result, more students lack basic information. In Granite Bay, one student asked where his cervix was, and another inquired if she could become pregnant from oral sex. Students in New York City protested that the increased focus on abstinence-only has curtailed access to education about HIV/AIDS. The Colorado Council of Black Nurses decided to return $16,000 in abstinence-only funding, because the program "was just too restrictive. It did not teach responsible sexual behavior."

Facts about abstinence-only education

• Over a five-year period ending in 2002, approximately $500 million in federal and state matching funds will have been spent on abstinence-only education. Because of the requirement that states match federal funds for abstinence-only programs, state dollars that previously supported comprehensive sexuality education—which includes but is not limited to abstinence-education—have been diverted to abstinence-only programs.

• The vast majority of American parents support comprehensive sex education. According to a recent study by the Kaiser Family Foundation, most parents want their children to receive a variety of information on subjects including contraception and condom use, sexually transmitted disease, sexual orientation, safer-sex practices, abortion, communications and coping skills, and the emotional aspects of sexual relationships. Given the choice, only 1% to 5% of parents remove their children from comprehensive sex education courses.

> *Students in comprehensive sex education classes do not engage in sexual activity more often or earlier.*

• Fewer than half of public schools in the U.S. now offer information on how to obtain birth control, and only a third include discussion of abortion and sexual orientation in their curricula. A large nationally representative survey of middle- and high-school teachers published in *Family Planning Perspectives* reported that 23% of teachers in 1999 taught abstinence as the *only* means of STD and pregnancy prevention, compared with 2% in 1988. The study's authors attributed the change to the heavy promotion of abstinence—not sound educational principles.

• Abstinence-only sex education doesn't work. There is little evidence that teens who participate in abstinence-only programs abstain from intercourse longer than others. When they do become sexually active, though, they often fail to use condoms or other contraceptives. Meanwhile, students in comprehensive sex education classes do not engage in sexual activity more often or earlier, but *do* use contraception and practice safer-sex more consistently when they become sexually active.

• The U.S. has the highest rate of teen pregnancy in the developed world, and American adolescents are contracting HIV faster than almost any other demographic group. The teen pregnancy rate in the U.S. is at least twice that in Canada, England, France, and Sweden, and 10 times that in the Netherlands. Experts cite restrictions on teens' access to comprehensive sexuality education, contraception, and condoms in the U.S., along with the widespread American attitude that a healthy adolescence should exclude sex. By contrast, the "European approach to teenage sexual activity, expressed in the form of widespread provision of confidential and accessible contraceptive services to adolescents, is . . . a central factor in explaining the more rapid declines in teenage childbearing in northern and western European countries."

• Every reputable sex-ed organization in the U.S., as well as prominent health organizations including the American Medical Association, have denounced abstinence-only sex ed. And a 1997 consensus statement from the National Institutes of Health concluded that legislation discouraging condom use on the ground that condoms are ineffective "places policy in direct conflict with science because it ignores overwhelming evidence. . . . Abstinence-only programs cannot be justified in the face of effective programs and given the fact that we face an international emergency in the AIDS epidemic."

Organizations to Contact

The editors have compiled the following list of organizations concerned with the issues debated in this book. The descriptions are derived from materials provided by the organizations. All have publications or information available for interested readers. The list was compiled on the date of publication of the present volume; names, addresses, phone and fax numbers, and e-mail addresses may change. Be aware that many organizations take several weeks or longer to respond to inquiries, so allow as much time as possible.

Advocates for Youth
2000 M St. NW, Suite 750, Washington, DC 20036
(202) 419-3420 • fax: (202) 419-1448
e-mail: questions@advocatesforyouth.org
Web site: www.advocatesforyouth.org

Advocates for Youth is the only organization that works both in the United States and in developing countries with a sole focus on adolescent reproductive and sexual health. It provides information, education, and advocacy to youth-serving agencies and professionals, policy makers, and the media. Among the organization's numerous publications are the fact sheets "Adolescent Protective Behaviors: Abstinence and Contraceptive Use" and "GLBTQ Youth: At Risk and Underserved," and the report *Science and Success: Sex Education and Other Programs That Work to Prevent Teen Pregnancy, HIV & Sexually Transmitted Infections*.

Alan Guttmacher Institute
120 Wall St., New York, NY 10005
(212) 248-1111 • fax: (212) 248-1951
e-mail: info@guttmacher.org • Web site: www.agi-usa.org

The institute works to protect and expand the reproductive choices of all women and men. It strives to ensure that people have access to the information and services they need to exercise their rights and responsibilities concerning sexual activity, reproduction, and family planning. Among the institute's publications are the special reports *Adding It Up: The Benefits of Investing in Sexual and Reproductive Health Care* and *U.S. Teenage Pregnancy Statistics*, and the fact sheet "Contraceptive Use— Teenagers' Sexual and Reproductive Health."

Centers for Disease Control and Prevention (CDC)
1600 Clifton Rd., Atlanta, GA 30333
(800) 311-3435 • fax: (770) 488-3110
e-mail: inquiry@cdc.gov • Web site: www.cdc.gov

The CDC is the federal agency charged with protecting the public health and safety at home and abroad by preventing and controlling diseases and by responding to public health emergencies. The CDC's At a Glance publications include *Assessing Health Risk Behaviors Among Young People: Youth Risk Behavior Surveillance System* and *Healthy Youth: An Investment in Our Nation's Future.*

Child Trends, Inc. (CT)
4301 Connecticut Ave. NW, Suite 100, Washington, DC 20008
(202) 572-6000 • fax: (202) 362-8420
e-mail: webmaster@childtrends.org • Web site: www.childtrends.org

CT works to provide accurate statistical and research information regarding children and their families in the United States and to educate the American public on the ways existing social trends, such as the rate of teenage pregnancy, affect children. In addition to the *Child Indicator* newsletter, which tracks children's well-being, CT also publishes the research briefs *Preventing Teenage Pregnancy, Childbearing and Sexually Transmitted Diseases: What the Research Shows* and *The First Time: Characteristics of Teens' First Sexual Relationships.*

Coalition for Positive Sexuality (CPS)
PO Box 77212, Washington, DC 20013-7212
(773) 604-1654
e-mail: cps@positive.org • Web site: www.positive.org

The Coalition for Positive Sexuality is a grassroots direct-action group formed in the spring of 1992 by high school students and activists. CPS works to counteract the institutionalized misogyny, heterosexism, homophobia, racism, and ageism that students experience every day at school. It is dedicated to offering teens education on sexuality and safe sex that is pro-woman, pro–lesbian/gay/bisexual, pro–safe sex, and pro-choice. Its motto is, "Have fun and be safe." CPS offers an online forum called "Let's Talk!" for teens to talk about sex.

Education World
1062 Barnes Rd., Suite 301, Wallingford, CT 06492
(203) 284-9330
e-mail: webmaster@educationworld.com
Web site: www.educationworld.com

Calling itself "the Educator's Best Friend," Education World's goal is to provide educators with a complete online resource for lesson plans and research materials. With 98 percent of the nation's public schools connected to the Internet, this resource provides information on how to integrate technology in the classroom. Education World publishes articles including "Kids Call Parents Heroes" and "Monitoring Children's Media Usage."

ETR Associates
4 Carbonero Way, Scotts Valley, CA 95066
(800) 321-4407 • fax: (800) 435-8433
e-mail: customerservice@etr.org • Web site: www.etr.org

ETR Associates, a private corporation, provides educational resources, training, and research in health promotion with an emphasis on sexuality and health education. It is the largest not-for-profit publisher of health education resources in the country. These resources include patient education pamphlets, posters, displays, newsletters, curricula, journals, books, and videos.

Family Research Council (FRC)
801 G St. NW, Washington, DC 20001
(202) 393-2100 • fax: (202) 393-2134
e-mail: corrdept@frc.org • Web site: www.frc.org

The council is a research, resource, and education organization that promotes the traditional family, which the council defines as a group of people bound by marriage, blood, or adoption. It opposes schools' tolerance of homosexuality and condom distribution programs in schools. It also believes that pornography breaks up marriages and contributes to sexual violence. Among the council's numerous publications is the Insight series of booklets which includes *Homosexuality and Child Sexual Abuse* and *Little Pills: Targeting Youth with New Abortion Drugs.*

Gay, Lesbian, and Straight Education Network (GLSEN)
121 W. Twenty-seventh St., Suite 804, New York, NY 10001
(212) 727-0135 • fax: (212) 727-0254
e-mail: glsen@glsen.org • Web site: www.glsen.org

GLSEN works to ensure safe and effective schools where every child learns to respect and accept all people, regardless of sexual orientation or gender/identity expression. GLSEN's online library holds many documents about creating safe schools including "That's So Gay," "Not Alone: Being a Straight Ally," and "Is This the Right School for Us?"

The Heritage Foundation
214 Massachusetts Ave. NE, Washington, DC 20002-4999
(202) 546-4400 • fax: (202) 546-8328
e-mail: info@heritage.org • Web site: www.heritage.org

The Heritage Foundation is a public policy research institute that supports the ideas of limited government and the free market system. It promotes the view that the welfare system has contributed to the problems of illegitimacy and teenage pregnancy. Among the foundation's numerous publications is its Backgrounder series, which includes "Government Spends $12 on Safe Sex and Contraceptives for Every $1 Spent on Abstinence," the analysis reports "Facts About Abstinence Education" and "Adolescents Who Take Virginity Pledges Have Lower Rates of Out-of-Wedlock Birth," and the commentary "Safe Sex: Time To Abstain."

iParenting Media
One Rotary Center, 1560 Sherman Ave., Evanston, IL 60201
(847) 556-2300
e-mail: media@iparentingmedia.com
Web site: www.iparentingmedia.com

iParenting Media employs the Internet, print, and radio in providing parents and parents-to-be with information about children from preconception through the teenage years. iParenting Media publishes the national magazine *Family Energy: Your Guide to a Fun and Fit Life with Kids* and online articles including "Straight Talk: Giving Your Child the Facts About Sex" and "Dating 101: Pre-dating Rituals for Your Teens."

Kaiser Family Foundation
2400 Sand Hill Rd., Menlo Park, CA 94025
(650) 854-9400 • fax: (650) 854-4800
e-mail: info@kaisernetwork.org • Web site: www.kaisernetwork.org

The Kaiser Family Foundation provides nonpartisan information on national health issues to policy makers, the media, and the general public. Their online resource features live webcasts of health policy events and produces three daily online reports: the *Kaiser Daily Health Policy Report*, the *Kaiser Daily HIV/AIDS Report*, and the *Kaiser Daily Reproductive Health Report*.

National Abortion and Reproductive Rights Action League (NARAL) Pro-Choice America
1156 Fifteenth St. NW, Suite 700, Washington, DC 20005
(202) 973-3000 • fax: (202) 973-3096
e-mail: can@ProChoiceAmerica.org • Web site: www.naral.org

NARAL Pro-Choice America is a grassroots organization formed to protect and defend a woman's right to choose. It works to reduce the need for abortions through better access to contraception, health care, and sex education. Among its publications are *Who Decides? A State-by-State Report on the Status of Women's Reproductive Rights* and *Talking About Freedom of Choice*.

National Campaign to Prevent Teen Pregnancy
1776 Massachusetts Ave. NW, Suite 200, Washington, DC 20036
(202) 478-8500 • fax: (202) 478-8588
e-mail: campaign@teenpregnancy.org
Web site: www.teenpregnancy.org

The mission of the National Campaign is to reduce teenage pregnancy by promoting values and activities that are consistent with a pregnancy-free adolescence. The campaign's goal is to reduce the pregnancy rate among teenage girls by one-third by the year 2005. The campaign publishes pamphlets, brochures, and opinion polls that include *No Easy Answers: Research Findings on Programs to Reduce Teen Pregnancy, Not Just for Girls: Involving Boys and Men in Teen Pregnancy Prevention*, and *Another Chance: Preventing Additional Births to Teen Mothers*.

National Organization on Adolescent Pregnancy, Parenting, and Prevention (NOAPPP)
509 Second St. NE, Washington, DC 20002
(202) 547-8814 • fax: (202) 547-8815
e-mail: noappp@noappp.org • Web site: www.noappp.org

NOAPPP promotes comprehensive and coordinated services designed for the prevention and resolution of problems associated with adolescent pregnancy and parenthood. It supports families in setting standards that encourage the healthy development of children through loving, stable relationships. NOAPPP publishes the quarterly *NOAPPP Network Newsletter* and various fact sheets on teen pregnancy.

Planned Parenthood Federation of America (PPFA)
434 W. Thirty-third St., New York, NY 10001
(212) 541-7800 • fax: (212) 245-1845
e-mail: communications@ppfa.org
Web site: www.plannedparenthood.com

Planned Parenthood believes individuals have the right to control their own fertility without governmental interference. It promotes comprehensive sex education and provides contraceptive counseling and services through clinics across the United States. Its publications include the brochures *A Young Woman's Guide to Sexuality, What if I'm Pregnant?* and *Is This Love? How to Tell if Your Relationship Is Good for You.*

Sexuality Information and Education Council of the United States (SIECUS)
130 W. Forty-second St., Suite 350, New York, NY 10036-7802
(212) 819-9770 • fax: (212) 819-9776
e-mail: siecus@siecus.org • Web site: www.siecus.org

SIECUS is an organization of educators, physicians, social workers, and others who support the individual's right to acquire knowledge of sexuality and who encourage responsible sexual behavior. The council promotes comprehensive sex education for all children that includes AIDS education, teaching about homosexuality, and instruction about contraceptives and sexually transmitted diseases. Its publications include fact sheets, annotated bibliographies by topic, and the monthly *SIECUS Report.*

Teen-Aid
723 E. Jackson Ave., Spokane, WA 99207
(509) 482-2868 • fax: (509) 482-7994
e-mail: teenaid@teen-aid.org • Web site: www.teen-aid.org

Teen-Aid is an international organization that promotes traditional family values and sexual morality. It publishes a public school sex education curriculum, *Sexuality, Commitment, and Family,* stressing sexual abstinence before marriage.

Bibliography

Books

Molly Barker   *Girls on Track*. New York: Ballantine, 2004.

Jane D. Brown,   *Sexual Teens, Sexual Media: Investigating Media's*
Jeanne R. Steele, and   *Influence on Adolescent Sexuality*. Mahwah, NJ:
Kim Walsh-Childers   L. Erlbaum, 2002.

Rhett Godfrey and   *The Teen Code: How to Talk to Us About Sex, Drugs,*
Neale S. Godfrey   *and Everything Else—Teenagers Reveal What Works*
    Best. Emmaus, PA: Rodale, 2004.

Janice M. Irvine   *Talk About Sex: The Battles over Sex Education in the*
    United States. Berkeley: University of California
    Press, 2002.

Joe Kelly   *Dads and Daughters: How to Inspire, Understand, and*
    Support Your Daughter When She's Growing Up So
    Fast. New York: Broadway, 2003.

Sharon Lamb   *The Secret Lives of Girls: What Good Girls Really*
    Do—Sex Play, Aggression, and Their Guilt. New York:
    Free Press, 2002.

Judith Levine and   *Harmful to Minors: The Perils of Protecting Children*
Joycelyn M. Elders   *from Sex*. Minneapolis: University of Minnesota
    Press, 2002.

Lynda Madaras   *What's Happening to My Body? Book for Boys:*
and Area Madaras   *A Growing Up Guide for Parents and Sons*. New York:
    Newmarket, 2000.

Lynda Madaras   *What's Happening to My Body? Book for Girls:*
and Area Madaras   *A Growing Up Guide for Parents and Daughters*. New
    York: Newmarket, 2000.

Josh McDowell   *The Disconnected Generation*. Nashville, TN: W,
    2000.

Josh McDowell   *Why True Love Waits: A Definitive Book on How to*
    Help Your Youth Resist Sexual Pressure. Carol Stream,
    IL: Tyndale, 2002.

Jay McGraw   *Life Strategies for Teens*. New York: Fireside, 2000.

Meg Meeker   *Epidemic: How Teen Sex Is Killing Our Kids*. Wash-
    ington, DC: Lifeline, 2002.

Debra J. Palardy   *Sweetie Here's the Best Reason on the Planet to Say No*
    to Your Boyfriend: Even If You've Already Said Yes.
    Pittsburgh, PA: Dorrance, 2000.

Lynn E. Ponton

The Sex Lives of Teenagers: Revealing the Secret World of Adolescent Boys and Girls. New York: Dutton, 2000.

Dennis Rainey, Barbara Rainey, and Steve Bjorkman

So You Want to Be a Teenager? What Every Preteen Must Know About Friends, Love, Sex, Dating, and Other Life Issues. Nashville, TN: Thomas Nelson, 2002.

Justin Richardson and Mark A. Schuster

Everything You Never Wanted Your Kids to Know About Sex, but Were Afraid They'd Ask: The Secrets to Surviving Your Child's Sexual Development from Birth to the Teens. New York: Crown, 2003.

Ritch C. Savin-Williams

Mom, Dad, I'm Gay: How Families Negotiate Coming Out. Washington, DC: American Psychological Association, 2001.

Meg Schneider

The Rules for Teens. New York: Scholastic, 2000.

Pam Stenzel and Crystal Kirgiss

Sex Has a Price Tag. Grand Rapids, MI: Zondervan, 2003.

Rebecca St. James

Wait for Me: Rediscovering the Joy of Purity in Romance. Nashville, TN: Nelson, 2003.

Leora Tanenbaum

Slut! Growing Up Female with a Bad Reputation. New York: Seven Stories, 1999.

Deborah L. Tolman

Dilemmas of Desire: Teenage Girls Talk About Sexuality. Cambridge, MA: Harvard University Press, 2002.

Periodicals

Arthur Allen

"Does 'Safe Sex' Really Exist?" *Salon*, July 21, 2000.

Renee Bacher

"Don't Make My Mistake: Straight Talk About Teen Sex from a State Senator," *Family Circle*, June 18, 2002.

Olivia Bayley

"Improvement of Sexual and Reproductive Health Requires Focusing on Adolescents," *Lancet*, September 6, 2003.

Nina Bernstein

"Young Love, New Caution; Behind Fall in Pregnancy, a New Teenage Culture of Restraint," *New York Times*, March 7, 2004.

Jane Brody

"Finding What Works in Sex Education," *San Diego Union-Tribune*, June 7, 2004.

Ruth S. Buzi et al.

"Gender Differences in the Consequences of a Coercive Sexual Experience Among Adolescents Attending Alternative Schools," *Journal of School Health*, May 2003.

Christian Century Foundation

"Teens Break No-Sex Vows, Study Suggests; Some Say Oral Sex Not Sex," *Christian Century*, December 27, 2003.

Carolyn L. Clawson and Marla Reese-Weber	"The Amount and Timing of Parent-Adolescent Sexual Communication as Predictors of Late Adolescent Sexual Risk-Taking Behaviors," *Journal of Sex Research*, August 2003.
Deborah A. Cohen et al.	"When and Where Do Youths Have Sex? The Potential Role of Adult Supervision," *Pediatrics*, December 2002.
Cynthia Harper et al.	"Adolescent Clinic Visits for Contraception: Support from Mothers, Male Partners, and Friends," *Perspectives on Sexual and Reproductive Health*, January/February 2004.
Jennifer L. Kornreich et al.	"Sibling Influence, Gender Roles, and the Sexual Socialization of Urban Early Adolescent Girls," *Journal of Sex Research*, February 2003.
Susan J. Landers	"Drugs, Alcohol and Unprotected Sex, Teen Cocktail of Choice: Physicians Are Urged to Help Steer Their Teen and Young Adult Patients Away from Destructive Behavior by Using Incisive Questions and Straight Answers," *American Medical News*, March 18, 2002.
Paige D. Martin et al.	"Expressed Attitudes of Adolescents Towards Marriage and Family Life," *Adolescence*, Summer 2003.
Molly Masland	"Carnal Knowledge: The Sex Ed Debate," *MSNBC Children's Health*, October 15, 2003.
Karl E. Miller	"Preventing Risky Sexual Behaviors in Adolescents," *American Family Physician*, October 1, 2002.
Jodie Morse	"An Rx for Teen Sex: Doctors Are Joining the Abstinence Movement. Here's Why They're Now Telling Kids, 'Just Say No,'" *Time*, October 7, 2002.
National Campaign to Prevent Teen Pregnancy	"Teens Tell All About . . . Advice to Friends About Sex," April 8, 2002.
National Campaign to Prevent Teen Pregnancy	"Thinking About the Right Now: What Teens Want Other Teens to Know About Preventing Teen Pregnancy," April 4, 2002.
Joyce Howard Price	"Teens Want to Wait for Sex," *Washington Times*, December 17, 2003.
Richard H. Schwartz and Regina Milteer	"Beach Week: Sand and Swimming or Sex and Swilling?" *Contemporary Pediatrics*, April 2001.
Mary B. Short and Susan L. Rosenthal	"Helping Teenaged Girls Make Wise Sexual Decisions," *Contemporary OB/GYN*, May 2003.
Society for the Advancement of Education	"Teen Sex Linked to Early Friendships," *USA Today*, April 2003.

TB & Outbreaks Week	"Report Finds No Evidence That Abstinence-Only Counseling Prevents Teen Sex, Pregnancy, Disease," May 21, 2002.
Teen People	"The Teen People Sex Survey: What Happens When You Stop Being Polite and Start Talking Openly About the Things You Do Behind Closed Doors? We Asked Everything . . . and You Answered! Warning: Some Stuff May Shock You, but It's All the Real Deal. Read on to Find Out How You and Your Friends Think, Act, and Feel When It Comes to S-E-X," November 1, 2003.
Linda Villarosa	"More Teenagers Say No to Sex, but Experts Aren't Sure Why," *New York Times*, December 3, 2003.
Kerri Wachter	"Epstein-Barr Virus Risk and Teen Sex," *Pediatric News*, January 2003.
Women's Health Weekly	"Emergency Contraceptive Availability Doesn't Boost Rate of Teen Unprotected Sex," April 22, 2004.
Michael Young et al.	"Religious Influence on the Sexual Behavior of Rural Youth," *Research Quarterly for Exercise and Sport*, March 2003.
Kate Zernike	"Teenagers Want More Advice from Parents on Sex, Study Says," *New York Times*, December 16, 2003.

Index

Aahung group, 50
abortions, 19, 87–88
abstinence, 15, 26, 28
  career goals and, 35–36
  controversy over, 32
  masturbation and, 27
  for pregnancy prevention 9–10, 17
  rings, 38–39
  role of religion in, 32–33, 37
  school programs and, 17, 99–100, 106–109
  secondary, 37–40
  society and, 34, 96
  spokesmen for, 37
  see also abstinence-only programs; virginity; virginity pledges
abstinence-only programs
  aggressiveness of, 33
  as best way to prevent sexual activity, 9–10
  endanger students, 104–109
  funding for, 32, 72, 105–106
  information about contraceptives and, 9, 16–18
  success of, 96, 99–102
  see also sex education; *and specific programs*
Ad-Health survey. *See* National Longitudinal Survey of Adolescent Health
Adolescent Family Life Act, 105
Adolescent Health Study (1997), 103
advertising, influence of, 81–82
Advocate (magazine), 65
Advocates for Youth program, 32
AIDS (acquired immune deficiency syndrome), 9, 24, 107, 109
  see also HIV
Alan Guttmacher Institute, 13, 20, 63, 88, 93–94
Albert, Bill, 11
alcohol, 24
Ali, Lorraine, 31
Allen, Claude, 15
Altman, Drew, 83
American Civil Liberties Union (ACLU), 105
American Family Association, 67
American Medical Association (AMA), 92
anal sex

condom use and, 51
is not real sex, 12, 15
presents greatest risk of HIV transmission, 51
statistics on, 63
appearance, virginity and, 36–38
Art of Loving Well Project, The, 102

Bearman, Peter, 41–43
Best, Kim, 45
birth control. *See* contraceptives
Blum, Robert, 25–26
Blumenfeld, Warren, 70
Boy Meets Girl (Harris), 37
boys
  attention from, 36
  media influence over, 81–82
  oral sex and, 22, 24
  risk of acquiring STDs for, 50–51
  self-esteem and sex, 18
  sexual misconceptions and, 50–51
Brown, Sarah, 24
Bruckner, Hannah, 41–43
Buckel, David, 68
Bulion, Leslie, 66

cable television. *See* television
Cameron, Kirk, 61, 65
Cameron, Paul, 64, 65
cancer, cervical, 47
career goals, abstinence and, 35–36
Cates, Willard, Jr., 46–47
censorship, 104–109
Centers for Disease Control and Prevention (CDC), 9, 13, 14, 32, 42, 98–99
cervical cancer, 47
cervix, 49
chancroid, 22
chastity. *See* abstinence
chastity law. *See* Adolescent Family Life Act
chastity pledges. *See* virginity pledges
chlamydia, 22, 49, 98
Choosing the Best program, 100–101
Christians, 32, 34, 105
Chunovic, Louis, 76
Clinton, Bill, 25
coitus. *See* sexual intercourse
condoms

sexual abuse, 51
sexual activity
  age of commencement of, 46
  coerced, 24, 51
  in developing countries, 50–51
  emotional health and, 53–59
  in European countries, 109
  negative consequences of, 9, 14–15,
    53–59, 97–98
  oral sex as part of, 20–30
  overview of teen, 12–19
  parental involvement and, 10–11
  prevention of, 9–11
  regrets about, 9, 19, 39–40, 53,
    57–58
  risky, 12–15, 47–48
  statistics on, 9, 12–13, 25, 53, 97
  trends in, 20–21, 32–33
  see also teen pregnancies; television
sexual intercourse
  coerced, 51
  expectations after, 12–13
  intimacy and, 33
  oral sex as an option to, 24–26
  readiness for, 33, 57, 84
  statistics on, 15, 32, 99–100
  virginity pledges and, 10
sexuality, control of, 35
Sexuality Information and Education
  Council, 9, 17, 99
sexually transmitted diseases (STDs)
  abstinence and, 9–10, 17
  boys and, 50–51
  complications from, 51–52
  condoms and, 16–17
  diagnosis of, 29, 52
  as an epidemic, 13–14, 45–52
  girls and, 49–50
  herpes, 12–13, 22–23, 52
  high rate of, in developing
    countries, 45
  oral sex and, 22–23, 29
  prevention of, 9
  risk factors for spread of, 46–47
  statistics on, 9, 13, 42–43, 53–54,
    91, 97–98
  treatment of, 45, 51–52
  see also AIDS; gonorrhea; HIV;
    human papilloma virus
Sexual Minority Advocacy Council
  (SMAC), 62
sexual-minority students. *See*
  homosexuality
sexual partners, multiple, 13, 98
sexual relations. *See* sexual
  intercourse
sexual revolution, 31, 64, 77
sex workers. *See* prostitutes

Sigma Project, 64
Silver Ring Thing, 38–39
single mothers. *See* teen mothers
society, influence of sex in, 34, 96
Stanford, John, 62
statistics
  on abortions, 88
  on chlamydia, 98
  on contraceptives, 93–94
  on depression, 55
  on herpes, 12–13
  on HIV, 9, 13–14, 45–46, 49
  on homosexuality, 61, 64
  on human papilloma virus (HPV),
    12–13, 98
  on oral sex, 12, 14, 21, 25
  on sexual activity, 9, 12–13, 25, 53,
    97
  on sexual intercourse, 15, 32,
    99–100
  on STDs, 9, 13, 42–43, 53–54, 91,
    97–98
  on teen pregnancies, 9, 13, 54, 88,
    91, 93–94, 101, 109
  on television, 78–79
  on virginity, 13
  on virginity pledges, 10, 16, 41–42,
    103
STDs. *See* sexually transmitted
  diseases
Steyer, James P., 10–11, 76
suicide, 54, 68
syphilis, 22, 52

Teen Advisors (group), 34
Teen-Aid, Inc. program, 101–102,
  105
teen birthrate, 13, 97, 99
teen mothers, 35, 54, 94–95, 97
teen pregnancies
  abortions and, 19
  costs of, 97
  decisions and, 19
  influence of television on, 73–74
  oral sex as a way to avoid, 20
  poverty and, 94–95
  prevention of, 9
  reasons for, 37, 109
  STDs and, 52
  statistics on, 9, 13, 54, 88, 91,
    93–94, 101, 109
television, 71–85
  cable channels, 77–78
  distorted sexual information
    provided by, 80–82
  increasing use of sex in
    programming, 77–79
  parental involvement and, 74–75,